SIMPLE RAISED BED AND CONTAINER GARDENING FOR SMALL SPACES

EASY URBAN HOMESTEAD FARMING METHODS TO GROW VEGETABLES, FRUIT, HERBS & PLANTS THIS SEASON!

JON MARRINER

HomesteadOffgridWorld.com

© Copyright Jon Marriner 2021 - All rights reserved.

The content contained within this book may not be reproduced, duplicated or transmitted without direct written permission from the author or the publisher.

Under no circumstances will any blame or legal responsibility be held against the publisher, or author, for any damages, reparation, or monetary loss due to the information contained within this book. Either directly or indirectly. You are responsible for your own choices, actions, and results.

Legal Notice:

This book is copyright protected. This book is only for personal use. You cannot amend, distribute, sell, use, quote or paraphrase any part, or the content within this book, without the consent of the author or publisher.

Disclaimer Notice:

Please note the information contained within this document is for educational and entertainment purposes only. All effort has been executed to present accurate, up to date, and reliable, complete information. No warranties of any kind are declared or implied. Readers acknowledge that the author is not engaging in the rendering of legal, financial, medical or professional advice. The content within this book has been derived from various sources. Please consult a licensed professional before attempting any techniques outlined in this book

By reading this document, the reader agrees that under no circumstances is the author responsible for any losses, direct or indirect, which are incurred as a result of the use of the information contained within this document, including, but not limited to, — errors, omissions, or inaccuracies.

CONTENTS

Introduction v

The Remarkable Advantages of Gardening 15

Getting Started
The Basics 27

Container Gardening
Gardening Almost Anywhere 49

Raised Bed Gardening
The Green Thumb Advantage 79

Vertical Gardening
A Trendy Alternative 113

Building Your Garden in a Small Space
Let's Do This! 135

Gardening Upkeep & Maintenance
A Little Goes a Long Way 155

Conclusion 175

Gardener's Terminology 177

Global Hardiness Zones 189

References 193

Design Space 195

A FREE GIFT FOR MY READERS

I have gathered **25 useful tips and tricks** that I use myself to help you get off to a great start and maintain a beautiful garden year after year.

- Tips for soaking seeds and speeding up germination time
- Recycle/repurpose household items to make gardening easier
- Rediscover an ancient soil amendment that will revitalize your vegetation!
- Pest control techniques
- **Plus, FREE printables and much more**!

www.HomesteadOffgridWorld.com

Be sure to join our members-only Facebook community to interact with beginner and experienced gardeners from around the world!
www.facebook.com/groups/homesteadoffgridworld

INTRODUCTION

Do you believe in magic? What if you knew there was a way to transform the smallest space into a beautiful, bountiful garden? Imagine stepping out of your home and into a natural paradise. Perhaps a canopy of leaves beckoning you to take a breather in the shade. Towering greenery along the edges, sheltering you from the outside world. A green, private nook just for you, the sunshine, and your fresh produce. Think of beautiful flowers bowing their charming heads in the sun, their fragrance hanging in the air like magic. Fresh herbs tumbling out of their containers, begging to visit your kitchen and swim in your stews. A few tomato plants heavy with juicy red fruits, warm from the kiss of the sun. Your small space *can* be magical. Yes, you *can* have all of this even *without* a large garden area! Contrary to popular belief, size does *not* matter! It isn't about how *much* space you have, but rather, how skillfully you *use* it.

This is the book for every type of gardener. Whether you are so new to gardening that you can't tell a rake from a spade, or whether you are an experienced gardener with years of dirt under your nails! You want to be introduced to the tools you need for gardening, or to the plants you can grow in your space, or to be inspired by new ideas. Maybe you want a short project to keep you busy for a while but don't want long and dreary steps to follow. You may even be interested in living off your own land but don't have much land to work with! You want a thriving garden in a small space, and you need tips and tricks to achieve that. Maybe you are on a mission to redesign your outdoor space — to give it a breath of fresh air and maximize your success in minimal square footage!

No matter where you are in the world of gardening, this is the book to help you get to where you want to be. This book covers every aspect of designing a garden in a limited space. It is about growing plants like the pros — transforming your outdoor space into something inviting, beautiful, or plentiful. It is also about easy and step-by-step instructions — clear and concise. Just follow the guidelines to start a garden, maintain your established garden, or grow more plants in your space than you ever imagined possible. Other "expert" gardening books are plain old boring textbooks! This book will help you *grow up* — as in literally, vertically! It will encourage you to look at the little landscape that you have available with a new perspective.

Consider this book a valuable source of information on planting arrangement, planning your planting, container gardening, raised bed gardening, pest control, fertilizing, general maintenance, and proven strategies and steps for designing a garden that will thrive on a minimal physical footprint. Learn how to group plants for maximum visual impact or prevent disease in the garden and win the war against the bad bugs. *Simple Raised Bed and Container Gardening for Small Spaces* is rich with tips and advice to help you find success in your garden adventures.

For some, gardening is a chore. For others, gardening is a hobby. But for folks like me, gardening is a passion! There's something satisfying about placing time, effort, and thought into cultivating the land. I am happiest in the heat of the sun, smelling the earth and nurturing the greens. It's been about fifteen years now, that I've really started getting serious about my gardening skills and picking up many tips and tricks along the way. I took on the challenge of learning all that I could about gardening in small spaces and container gardening to help others who are passionate about gardening. My vision is to guide gardeners on how to work with a small space. I took to writing this book to help people make the most of their room and achieve success in gardening without hiring professionals! There is so much joy in doing it yourself, and nothing compares to the pride you feel after completing a project as rewarding as a beautiful and abundant garden. I'm offering only the best information that is out there on space-saving gardening. I take the guesswork out of it for you so that you can focus on making your dream garden a reality. You can absolutely enjoy a productive garden. I am here to promise you that you can do this — from start to finish!

Simple Raised Bed and Container Gardening for Small Spaces will provide a gardener of any skill level with helpful information. It will also inspire you and evoke and feed a love for gardening and genuine appreciation for the practice itself. Gardening is an activity that requires thought, skill, and patience. It is about so much more than cleaning up the yard. If you are the type of gardener who simply yanks out a couple of weeds, tosses some dirt around, and stands with a hose in hand, then it's time to turn over a new leaf! You will certainly grow to love the feel of the soil, the beauty of every leaf, stem, and flower, and the simple pleasure of nurturing life while creating beauty.

Suppose you are already passionate about gardening and everything it has to offer both you and your piece of land. In that case, this book is still essential for getting the most out of your hobby. Whether you dream of leafy privacy, overflowing blossoms, or bountiful edibles, this is the book you will need to make it come to life. There is something gratifying about modifying the smallest piece of land into something amazing using your own two hands. The world of gardening is vast and practically limitless — brimming with an assortment of plants like shrubs, trees, bulbs, ferns, flowering plants, and even grasses. Together, we can make something amazing with the space that you have!

Who This Book is for?

Whether you've never watered a plant or whether you've single-handedly created a natural wonder in your back yard — or anything in between — this book is for you! That's because this is a gardening book full of all the best information for people who love plants. It has all the guidance a beginner needs, the refresher information for an intermediate gardener to benefit from, and the tips and tricks an experienced gardener is looking for. This is a book for anybody who appreciates gardening at any level.

How This Book Will Benefit You

After reading this book, you will know precisely what you need to grow healthy plants and have a flourishing garden, no matter the size or space you have. First-timers can learn how to develop a garden like a pro, what tools they will need to begin building a garden in a limited space, what to plant and where to plant it, and the basics of growing in containers and raised beds. Intermediate gardeners can upgrade their gardening skills and pick up new techniques to improve their gardens and care for their plants. This book also serves as a rich source of information for experienced gardeners on plant care, watering, climate conditions and growing seasons, tips and tricks for container and raised bed gardening, and garden maintenance and aftercare. With this book as a guide, you can have a beautiful and bountiful garden in the smallest of spaces and with any level of gardening skills.

Who is Jon Marriner?

For over 30 years, I've been dabbling in the garden and experimenting with learned techniques and local expertise to achieve a fantastic crop at the end of the season. In the last fifteen years I've really started ramping up my gardening skills and helping others with their gardening challenges. When I was a child, I remember gardening side by side with my father. I would ask him all kinds of questions and just watch him work. When my father passed away, my love of gardening grew as I felt connected to him when my hands were dirty. I've always had a love of homesteading and anything that comes with it. Gardening is such a passion of mine and I'm always trying to innovate and improve the experience. Doing so allows me to share my results with new and experienced green thumbs so that you can benefit as well. Of course, sometimes things don't work out the way I'd hoped. Gardening is never a perfect science! Whether it be an unusual growing season due to weather, pest nuisances, or just plain ol' bad luck, I've learned to experiment and adapt for the next growing seasons by utilizing my findings as well as expert tips and tricks to mitigate or eliminate these pesky issues altogether.

Book Layout

This book **begins** by introducing you to the amazing advantages of gardening. **Chapter two** is about what plants need to thrive and what tools are needed to make that happen. You will learn about the relationship between your environment and your garden and also learn the important questions you have to answer before you start digging!

The third and fourth chapters are an exciting journey! The **third chapter** takes you through container gardening — the kind of gardening that doesn't even require a garden bed. For gardeners with garden beds, **chapter four** is an informative chapter on raised bed gardening in small spaces. Here you learn about the different types of raised bed gardens, the mistakes you can avoid when raised bed gardening, and the many tips and tricks to follow to make your raised bed flourish.

The **fifth chapter** covers vertical gardening — an exciting concept that can completely transform a space. You will be introduced to many creative ways to grow your garden vertically and the benefits of this unconventional method of gardening. When you don't have much room, the solution is to plant upwards — the sky really *is* the limit in this case!

Chapter six focuses on small spaces and how you can build a garden in a space of any shape. You will be guided on how to design a showstopper of a garden in a limited space and many tips on how to achieve it successfully. Container gardening makes a beautiful garden a possibility even if you don't have a garden! Transform your balcony, driveway, or even a patch of concrete into a green paradise.

The book wouldn't be complete without the **final chapter** on maintenance and aftercare, helping you keep your garden healthy and thriving. It is a rich source of information on feeding your plants, protecting them from pests and disease, and keeping your outdoor space clean and tidy. This is important information for keeping your plants happy and disease-free so that you can enjoy them longer, and also for keeping your outdoor space neat and presentable so that you can enjoy the space to its fullest.

As a bonus, I have included a **Gardener's Terminology** section at the end of this book to help you build your gardening vocabulary! You'll also find an up-to-date **Hardiness Zone** section for North America, Europe, and Australia to help you identify the best plants to grow successfully in your region. I've created a **Design Space** section at the very back of this book where you can scribble, doodle, design, and jot down notes. I hope this will help you express your ideas and get you to achieve your end goal; to create your own garden you can be proud of!

Lastly, to help my readers from around the world enjoy this book to its full potential, I have done my best to ensure the sizes and measurements discussed within are in both US and metric units.

> Note: To save you money on this paperback, the photos have been printed in black and white. If you would like to view the photos in full color, please purchase the Kindle or Audible edition which will include a free color PDF.

It is a golden maxim to cultivate the garden for the nose, and the eyes will take care of themselves."

-by Robert Louis Stevenson

1

THE REMARKABLE ADVANTAGES OF GARDENING

The act of cultivating a patch of the earth, no matter how small, brings joy to the soul and the planet. Gardening is about scattering the tiniest of seeds and eagerly waiting for their little green heads to pop out of the dirt. It is a lifelong journey that meets no end. A beautiful and thriving garden is something appreciated by everyone. Yet, so few spare the time to discover the wonderful hobby of gardening. Gardeners know the feeling of joy in the dancing leaves of a happy plant and take pride in the colorful flower that peeps over the bushes to look at them!

Why Gardening?

When everything else in the world is frustrating, unstable, and in chaos, your garden can be a place of purity and peace — a natural reminder of the beauty of life. There's nothing like watching plants grow, flowers bloom, and fruits ripen to make you appreciate the magic of life. Gardening brings you down to earth. It brings you closer to Mother Nature. It activates the senses; you *see* the beautiful colors of the plants, taste the juicy tomato, feel the damp soil, hear the rustle of leaves in the wind, and smell the blooms' fragrance. So when answering the question, "why gardening?" you have to ask yourself, "why not?"

The Health Benefits of Gardening

The top reasons you should get down on your knees and get dirt under your nails are these. Gardening is a natural therapy. It calms the mind and quiets the loudest of thoughts. There's nothing like gardening to teach you the value of patience, hard labor, and determination, especially when those weeds start racing with your fingers as you pluck them out! Scrambling around the garden does wonders for your physical health, as does eating fresh organic produce. Cultivating your little land is a way to connect with nature. Here's a list of some of the ways that you can benefit from the activity of gardening.

Fight Disease and Build Immunity

Give disease a kick with the old garden boot! Getting your fingers in the soil exposes your body to friendly bacteria that live in the garden. These good bugs are your body's warriors in the war against asthma, allergies, psoriasis, and more! Spending time in the sun also builds your immune system, thanks to vitamin D. Just as a plant synthesizes chlorophyll in the sunlight, your body synthesizes vitamin D when your skin is exposed to sunlight. Vitamin D is an essential nutrient that your body relies on for hundreds of functions. It has been proven that exposure to sunlight lowers an individual's risk of many diseases, including bladder, breast and colorectal cancer, multiple sclerosis, and non-Hodgkin's lymphoma[1]. Too much of a good thing is always a bad thing, so all things considered, avoid overexposure to the sunlight when its rays are at their harshest.

Improves Moods

Speaking of the good bugs, did you know that healthy bacteria live in your garden soil that you actually inhale? Inhaling these good guys makes your body release serotonin and reduces anxiety, improving your mood. The next time you breathe in the dust as you dig up your garden, know that you'll be smiling wider afterward! Chucking soil around has time and again helped people fight depression and increase their self-esteem. Because, how couldn't a pretty flower put a smile on your face?

Build Physical Strength

Carrying around the spade, spearing the dirt with your fork, and pushing around the wheelbarrow — some of the many movements that help you grow stronger and healthier! All that prodding, pulling, and planting keeps your arms and hands strong while squatting and walking does wonders for the legs and posture! Gardening is a workout — whether the athletes agree or not. The *Centers for Disease Control and Prevention* declares gardening as an exercise, and anybody who has spent a couple of hours doing yard work will agree. Garden work employs every major muscle group; the soreness you feel the day after a good gardening session will confirm it! Vitamin D is another hero in the aspect of strength. It builds and maintains stronger bones by increasing the uptake of calcium by the body[2].

Improving Memory and Mental Performance

The fact that gardening improves cognitive function is no secret in the medical community. Recent evidence is supportive of the idea that gardening results in the growth of memory-related nerves in the brain. There's a term for using gardening as a mental health improvement tool — horticultural therapy (and it's been around *forever*). Extensive research has been done on the effect of gardening on dementia patients, and the outcome is groundbreaking. Of course, you don't need to have dementia to receive the same neurological benefits from spending time in the garden.

Stress-Busting

Cortisol is a notorious stress hormone that leads to many unwanted effects in the body, including but not limited to excessive weight gain, elevated blood pressure, and osteoporosis. Spending time in the garden has proven to reduce cortisol levels and aid in recovery from stressful events. The release of endorphins during gardening activities also aids in uplifting spirits and counteracting stress. You have to admit; there's nothing like hammering into the ground with a hoe or shovel to release tension! You are deserving of calmness and peace of mind — get out in the garden and seize it!

Aids Addiction Recovery

It's strongly believed that plants are the perfect friends to people recovering from drug or alcohol addiction. Studies have uncovered that working with plants evoked positive feelings in recovering addicts, resulting in the completion of their recovery program faster and more effectively. In fact, the activity of gardening showed greater improvement in patients than artwork did!

Fosters Human Connections

Those who garden together grow together! Gardening with others is proven to foster better and stronger, more satisfying relationships with others. Gardening is a suggested activity for schools, communities, and families to drive a sense of well-being and to help expand personal and social growth. Also, when you're out in the garden, there's a high chance you will strike up a conversation with passers-by and neighbors — conversation is the paving to friendship. Having regular interactions with others improves well-being and overall satisfaction.

Heals and Empowers

Gardening can nurture your soul. Your garden can be a private space for tranquility and peace. It is an escape from the demands of daily life. Beautiful blooms lift the spirits while yanking out those weeds are a welcome release of tension. Sinking your teeth into fresh produce that you have grown with your own two hands is deeply satisfying. The simple act of nurturing a seedling into a strong and healthy plant is rewarding to the spirit. Having the knowledge and skills to use the land to grow food is empowering. There's something magical in sowing a tiny seed and helping it grow into a big harvest.

Combats Eco-anxiety

Feelings of anxiety over the future of our planet are now a very common experience. The generations of today place environmental and ecological concerns at the forefront. For example, a person who wants to do their share in saving a little piece of the earth, looking after pollinators by growing plants that attract them is one way of taking action. Growing a plant is about more than the plant; it's about the insects that depend on its pollen, the microorganisms that depend on its roots, and the critters that depend on its spent leaves. Gardening is a way to do kind to nature and make the world a little better to live in. You don't have to cultivate acres of land to make a difference. A small wildflower patch will bring plenty of happiness to the bees and the butterflies, too!

Garden to Learn

Anyone who has spent some time getting to know their plants and their soil will tell you that it's only a matter of time before you want to know more and more! There's always an opportunity to learn when it comes to matters of the garden. From choosing what plants to grow and when, identifying pests and diseases, and understanding each

plant's needs to help them thrive. It's an ongoing and never-ending process — an activity you can never grow bored with! Plants are sort of like people, with each kind of plant having its own needs and likes. Learning which plants need full sun or shade, which need sandy soil or rich soil, which need infrequent watering, and which prefer their feet dry, is all part of the gardening experience. Beginning a journey in gardening is beginning a lifelong journey.

Garden to Make Money

While gardening is rewarding in a multitude of ways, it can also be financially rewarding. The soil can serve you financially whether you grow on acres of land to sell to the markets, whether you work for a garden center, or whether you simply slash your grocery bill by growing fresh produce for your dinner table. If you grow enough of a harvest, you could even sell some of your fruits and vegetables to friends and neighbors. Not to mention, a beautiful garden adds value to your property, and real estate agents have approximated that an attractive landscape can see your value rise by up to 15%! For the passionate entrepreneur, gardening can manifest into a profitable independent business. Many plants are easily propagated, with the only cost to you being a baggie and some soil, offering an excellent opportunity to make money from cloning your plants! Sell seedlings and established cuttings at below-nursery prices for a handsome profit. Allow plants to set seeds and collect seeds for selling to others. Another easy way to make money almost effortlessly from your garden is to save cuttings of herbs when pruning your plants and sell these cheaper than the supermarkets. You could consider drying herbs and flowers and making potpourri mixes or scented oils etc. The opportunities are endless!

Garden to Meet People

Reach out to like-minded people by chatting about plants, sharing some bulbs, or exchanging fresh produce. Gardening presents the opportunity for great social interaction because there's so much to talk about and so much to do! An in-person or online gardening group is a great way to share information, ask questions, get ideas about gardening, and improve the health of your plants or the beauty of your garden.

> Want a place to start connecting with other like-minded gardeners? Then come check out our exciting Facebook group at **_Homestead and Off-Grid World_** and join our friendly community! You can also sign up for our newsletter and connect to our group that way at
> www.HomesteadOffgridWorld.com

Garden to be Creative

Like art, gardening is a means of expressing creativity. Your imagination is the limit when transforming a space using soil, plants, rocks, and grasses. Put your creative pants on and go out and have fun! Design a space using different leaves, blooms, grasses, or arrangements of stones and pavers. Decorate and pattern the earth with a variety of ferns and shrubs. Dive into a DIY sculpture or make some planters, a couple of pavers, or even a few cute gnomes. A garden is a place for experimenting with colors, textures, and themes. You can make something beautiful from something plain, and all it takes is your two hands, this book, and a few tools. Consider your garden the canvas, and you, the artist! There is always room for creativity, and the smaller your space, the more creative you have to be to decorate and transform it.

Rooftop gardens in an urban setting.

2

GETTING STARTED

The Basics

The goal of any gardener, no matter what type of garden they are growing, is to make their plants smile. Your plants will be happiest when all their needs are met. In this section of the book, we take a good look at just what they need and why. This is a good read for every gardener!

What Plants Want and Need

There are five basic needs that have to be met for your plants to grow to their best — light, air, water, nutrients, and space. This section takes a deeper look at each of these requirements and how and why they are important.

Sun & Air

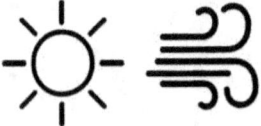
The very concept of photosynthesis is a magical one. The idea of a living thing harnessing natural light to manufacture its own starches and sugars to grow. Plants use the energy from the sunshine to convert non-mineral elements from the air into food that the plant's tissues absorb. Most fruits and vegetables require direct sunlight to grow. As a gardener, you do not have control over the amount of carbon, hydrogen, and oxygen in the air that your plants use, but you do have control over their exposure to sunlight. Any plant producing food must receive many hours of direct sunlight, with most plants requiring a minimum of six hours. Plants can be grown under artificial light, which is done in indoor gardening and small-scale indoor farming. As an average gardener, you could use artificial light to grow your seedlings ahead of time, for example. Without enough light, a plant's growth is stunted. On the other extreme, too much light can lead the plant and the soil it grows in to dry out. Knowing how much or how little light your plants need is important for healthy, strong growth. Improper light conditions don't spell instant death, though! A lack of light results in gangly stems, poor blossoming and blooms of pale color, pale leaves, and a generally unhappy plant. Too much light appears as sunburn and brown spots on the leaves, wilting and drying leaf tips. Here's an interesting fact: if the sun would stop burning for some reason, most plants would

invariably die from the cessation of photosynthesis. Still, some trees can survive for decades without any sunshine!

Water

We know that plants need water, but what for? For one, the process of photosynthesis requires water molecules to manufacture food. Secondly, water acts in plants much the same way blood does in humans and animals — it transports nutrients from the soil through the plant right to the tips of its leaves. Various plants require different amounts and frequencies of watering. Some plants prefer wet feet, while others need to let their feet dry between waterings! Too little water, and your plants may shrivel up and die. Too much water and their roots may rot — so they die! It's a bad ending either way.

Nutrients and Soil

There are sixteen elements essential for a well-nourished plant. These elements are categorized as either mineral or non-mineral elements. The soil is a typical plant's source of nutrients. The three primary nutrients are nitrogen, potassium, and phosphorus, which dissolve in water and are taken up by the plant's root system. If you are growing plants in poor soil, fertilizer helps provide nourishment to accelerate plant growth. Another method of ensuring that sufficient nutrients are present in the soil is to practice crop rotation (an advanced planting strategy). Plants also require specific ranges of acidity or alkalinity to flourish. Most plants prefer a range between a pH of 6.1 and 7.0. Unfortunately, there's no way of knowing whether your soil is fertile by simply eyeballing it. The good news is that there are DIY testing kits that are simple to use to find out whether your soil is alkaline or acidic. The risk of incorrect pH levels includes high acidity, ill-affecting the growth of beneficial bacteria, and high alkalinity limiting plants' access to minerals.

Space

Plants generally like some room to wiggle their toes. The roots of a plant travel in the soil, some deeper than others so that they can spread out and search for sufficient nutrients and moisture. The leaves also need space so that they can capture the sunlight to photosynthesize. Growing plants too closely together means that their root systems or leaves have to compete for resources, placing strain on the plants and thus not allowing them to grow to their full potential.

Balanced Environment

Successful gardening is about striking the right balance between plants' needs and the environment it grows in. Here we take a closer look at the environment your plants will be growing in — climate, seasons, location, and general space.

Temperatures and Climate

The influence of temperature begins with a seed. Germination occurs at different temperatures for different plants. Naturally, cool-season crops require low temperatures to sprout, while warm-weather crops prefer higher temperatures to sprout. Once the plant has grown, temperature changes will affect photosynthesis, respiration and transpiration, vegetative growth, and reproductive growth. Temperature also affects the storage of sugars and starches in plants. Understanding a plant's temperature requirements puts you in a better position to improve its health considerably, especially in conditions where the temperature is easily manipulated, such as indoor gardening.

Climate is important for the simple reason that your outdoor plants have to be compatible with the climate they are to grow in. Consider the humidity, rainfall, summer and winter temperatures, and the length of the growing season. The different climate types are tropical, dry, temperate, continental, and polar. Hardiness zone maps are an important tool for gardeners to know which plants can survive outdoors according to their specific region. I have included these maps in the "Global Hardiness Zones" section at the end of this book. Knowing the zone you are in is very helpful for selecting certain plants that are picky about their growing climate.

Growing Seasons

This is exactly what it sounds like — growing seasons are the seasons during which a plant grows. Planting dates vary for different fruits and vegetables. Growing plants in the correct season is one factor that allows the plants to grow their best and yield their maximum. The two general growing seasons are cool-season and warm-season crops.

Hardy vegetables may be planted two to four weeks before the last sign of frost. They germinate in cold soil, and the little seedling that pokes out of the ground can withstand short freezes. Examples are broccoli, garlic, kohlrabi, asparagus, collards, onions, cabbage, horseradish, leeks, Brussels sprouts, turnips, peas, spinach, rhubarb, rutabagas, and parsley.

Half-hardy crops germinate in cold soil, but the seedlings cannot tolerate much of a chill. These are best planted at the time of the last frost to avoid extended freezing temperatures. Examples are endive, globe artichokes, chard, carrots, potatoes, lettuce, beetroots, Chinese cabbage, chard, parsnips, cauliflower, chicory, and celery.

Tender crops are warm-weather crops that are best planted one or two weeks after the date of the last frost. Examples are sweet corn, tomatoes, New Zealand spinach, and snap beans.

Very tender crops are the second category of warm weather crops, best planted later than tender crops, at least three weeks after the date of the last frost. Examples are eggplant, peppers, cucumbers, okra, lima beans, sweet potatoes, muskmelons, pumpkins, watermelons, and squash.

Locations

Not only do you have to decide *what* to plant, but you also have to decide *where* to plant it. Do you want to garden outdoors in the warm sunshine? Do you want to have an indoor garden that places more control in your hands? Do you want to share your garden with others? Do you want to take on the exciting challenge of gardening in a small space? This section will help you make a choice!

Outdoors vs. Indoors

Indoor gardening puts a lot more control in the hands of the gardener than outdoor gardening does. Weather is unpredictable, even if you do follow the climate charts and carefully select your plants. When gardening indoors, you have control over the amount of water, lights, and nutrients that your plants receive. Indoor gardening is about sheltering your plants from harsh outdoor conditions. It allows you to garden even when the weather is poor outside. Also, with indoor gardening, your plants are safe from pests and wild animals, like rodents, birds, and insects. Growing plants indoors is also immensely convenient compared to outdoor gardening.

Outdoor gardening presents a welcome challenge for gardeners who like working with Mother Nature — even though she does have mood swings! Gardening outdoors is a lot of fun, and there are devices and techniques to help your plant survive destructive winds, temperature fluctuations, and pests. Fencing can act as a windbreaker. Mulching, cold frames, and row covers help protect from frost and cold weather. Netting offers shade from harsh sunlight and retains moisture.

Community Gardening

There is definitely space somewhere for a community garden to thrive. Whether on public or private land, a community garden brings many benefits. Sharing a plot of land to grow food means that many people are involved in the garden's success. The skills, knowledge, and workforce of a group of people far exceed the capabilities of a single person. Growing food in a community garden means you can harvest various foods with a fraction of the work since everyone is pitching in.

Small Space Options

The potential of the smallest spaces is astonishing! Land of any shape, soil, and size can be home to an array of plants. For the land that has the poorest soil, or even a complete lack of it, there's a raised bed gardening. For the narrowest and smallest spaces, there is vertical gardening. And finally, you would be hard-pressed to find a plant that cannot be grown in a container garden!

Containers

Container gardening offers versatility, accessibility, mobility, and flexibility. Growing plants in containers allow you to move them around freely, control their soil pH and nutrition, cater for different water needs, and control the space around your plants. An added advantage is minimal weeding and not needing heavy and bulky gardening tools and equipment. You could just turn the soil over in a pot with a kitchen fork — though you will get weird stares!

Raised Beds

Raised garden beds are mounds of soil above the grade of the ground, contained by some structure, often wood or brick. This method of gardening allows you to control soil health, enables more convenient access to the garden beds, and is generally aesthetically appealing. The elevated bed keeps many pests from affecting your plants as well. They also offer better drainage. This is one of the easiest forms of gardening and so is best for beginners. The many benefits make it an attractive method for intermediate and experienced gardeners alike.

Vertical

Increasing your growing space in a limited square area is as simple as growing vertically. Vertical structures offer beauty by adding height and depth to a space. Vertical gardening can be used to increase privacy. Plants are more accessible to grow in this method. They love stretching out, reaching for the sky. The improved air circulation of this method also leads to happier plants and healthier growth. Training climbers to grow upwards also frees up space on the ground, where you can grow even more.

Important Considerations

Here we have a few important questions to ask yourself to help you plan your garden. Answering these questions will give you some direction with your garden and help you feel more confident in your choices as you go about building your new garden or reinventing your old one!

What types of plants do you want to grow?

Are you gardening to beautify your outdoor space, or are you gardening to bring fresh produce to your kitchen table? Knowing whether your garden is ornamental or functional is important before you set out. Of course, you can have them both — a garden as pleasing to the eye as it is to the stomach!

If food gardening, what do you like to cook with and eat?

It only makes sense that you should grow the foods you enjoy eating — the foods you use most frequently in your kitchen. Plant the fruits you enjoy blitzing in your morning smoothie or the variety of tomatoes you most enjoy in your sauces. Plant the salad greens that you find most delicious!

How much space and light is there available for your gardening space?

The amount of sunlight your yard receives changes throughout the day, as the sun moves through the sky and shadows are cast in different directions. Get started with your garden by keeping a record of the amount of sunlight your yard receives. Keep an eye on the light pattern every two hours over the day, and note where the shadows fall and how many hours of sunlight each area receives. Observe the shadows cast by buildings and walls. Sketch the outline of your yard on sketching paper and use tracing paper to mark off the shaded areas every two hours. After some time, you will have enough data to use markers like pegs, flags, or stakes to indicate areas of shade, full sun, and partial sun.

Other Factors

How much time are you willing to spend in the garden? Some plants require higher maintenance than others. Will you be fussing over the plants, pruning them, and preening them a couple of hours a week? Or will you be spending time in the dirt only every two or three weeks?

Assess your landscape and visualize your finished garden as you would like it to look. You may have some bushes or plants already growing in the garden. You will have to decide whether you want these plants to form part of the garden you are building. Decide on the financial investment you are willing to make into the garden, as you will know whether to choose low-maintenance plants and planting methods or whether you will maintain more demanding plants and planting techniques.

How to Water Plants

Why do we water plants? Because they get thirsty, of course! You would think that watering your plants is a no-brainer, but there's more to it than you first thought! Fortunately, there are some golden rules to follow when watering plants and a few simple techniques that you can follow to get it right. Firstly, always water after repotting a plant. Next, know that plants in containers dry out faster than those in garden beds. Of course, the smaller the pot, the faster the soil dries out. Needless to say, the more sunlight a plant receives, the faster its moisture dries out. And finally, a higher humidity maintains moisture in the soil longer than low humidity.

Watering your plants isn't rocket science, and neither is it a chore! Do not schedule watering time because different plants have different requirements, just like different sized pots dry out at different rates and different soils have different retention rates! Here are the basics of watering your plants.

Frequency

Understanding the native climate of your plants will help you know their water requirements. For example, cacti grow in the desert — a dry place that barely receives water. So naturally, keeping your cactus' feet wet is not going to make for a happy cactus! Plants with fat, juicy leaves are full of water, so they do not require frequent watering and prefer a good soak after being allowed to dry out sufficiently. Plants with thin, delicate leaves typically require frequent watering, with moist (not wet) soil, like ferns.

Test to see if plants need water

When uncertain, it helps to know that most plants prefer the soil to dry out a bit before the next watering. The key here is not to let the soil dry out until it is bone dry, at which point it begins to repel water rather than absorb it like a sponge. You can't just tell by eye whether a plant needs water or not. Sometimes the surface of the soil appears dry, but there is moisture beneath the surface.

> **Pro Tip:** To test the soil and determine whether it is time for the next watering, insert a finger into the soil approximately 2 inches (5 cm) deep, and feel for moisture. Once the soil dries to this depth, your plant will be thirsty and gladly accept a drink!

Sprinkle rather than dump water

Think about when you are thirsty. You prefer to sip your water rather than have it poured onto your face, right? Well, plants are much the same. They prefer to absorb water slowly and steadily through their roots and don't particularly appreciate water being thrown all over them. In fact, many plants have a protective coating on their leaves that protects them from exposure to water, preventing fungal infections. Some plants benefit from the humidity offered by the wet leaves, but it is best to water their roots well and focus on doing this correctly.

To water your plants, use tepid water to saturate the soil with small additions at a time until fully saturated. Do not dump water into the pot of the plant and call it a day!

Affected by type of soil

Once water is added to the soil, it travels through the air spaces in the soil where it either drains, gets taken up by plant roots, or evaporates. Soil type is categorized into three categories, and then a combination of sand, clay, and loam. The texture of your soil determines its relationship with water. Sand is coarse and the largest particle of the three. Silt is fine and feels like flour. Clay is practically dust-like and is the type boasting the smallest particles. Clay soils are sticky when wet and do not drain well but are rich in nutrients. The other extreme is sandy soils, which drain too fast and are low in nutrients.

Equipment

If you're new to the gardening scene, you may get excited and think you must have every tool you lay eyes on! This is not the case. You can have a beautiful, thriving garden without 1001 tools. The most effective strategy for a beginner is to focus on purchasing high-quality tools that are multifunctional and necessary. In addition to the tools below, invest in a good wide-brimmed garden hat, strong gloves, and knee pads so that you don't have any excuses not to go out and get into the garden!

The tools you need will change as your gardening skills change. Right here is a barebones list of tools to get you started:

Gardening Gloves	While one of the best contact points to earth is our bare skin, some plants and creepy crawlies will want to bite back. Protect yourself with the right pair of gloves for hours of comfort in the garden.	
Small shovel or trowel	A simple, small shovel is all you need. Use this to dig out weeds and stumps, transplant your plants and dig holes. This is a tool that you will turn to most regularly, especially at the start of building your garden.	
Hoe (for bigger gardens)	There are many types of hoes to choose from, but they all serve the same purpose. Choose a long-handled hoe with a paddle head — this is the easiest version to use, helping you dislodge tough weeds or shape mounds of soil.	
Pruning Shears	Hand pruners, also called secateurs, will come in handy once your plants take off and start to take over.	
Garden Fork	An efficient tool for turning up soil. This tool can help loosen dense soil better than a spade.	

Watering Can

Choose a watering can that holds a large capacity but is not large enough that you will struggle to lug it around when it is full. Ensure that the handle is comfortable to grip and that the water won't spill out easily from the brim. A long angular neck gives much-needed reach, while a removable rosette sprinkler head offers more control over the flow. Note that plastic watering cans will not last you as long as a metal constructed can will — even the heavy-duty plastic kind. If you want to get fancy, some watering cans come fitted with a mister!

Know Your Soil

Your soil will be a mixture of sand, silt, and clay. To find out what type of soil you have, simply fill a jar two-thirds full of water and then add enough soil to fill the jar. Adding a little dish soap can help to separate the soil components. Shake the jar vigorously and then leave it undisturbed for a few days. After about five days, closely examine the layers that have formed. There should be three layers — sand settles to the bottom, silt sits on top, and clay remains suspended in the water above the silt. Estimate the percentage of the jar of each of these layers. Now use the diagram[3] below to find out what type of soil you have. The diagram is a useful guide on mixing the soil you want if you make up your garden soil from scratch.

Soil Textural Triangle

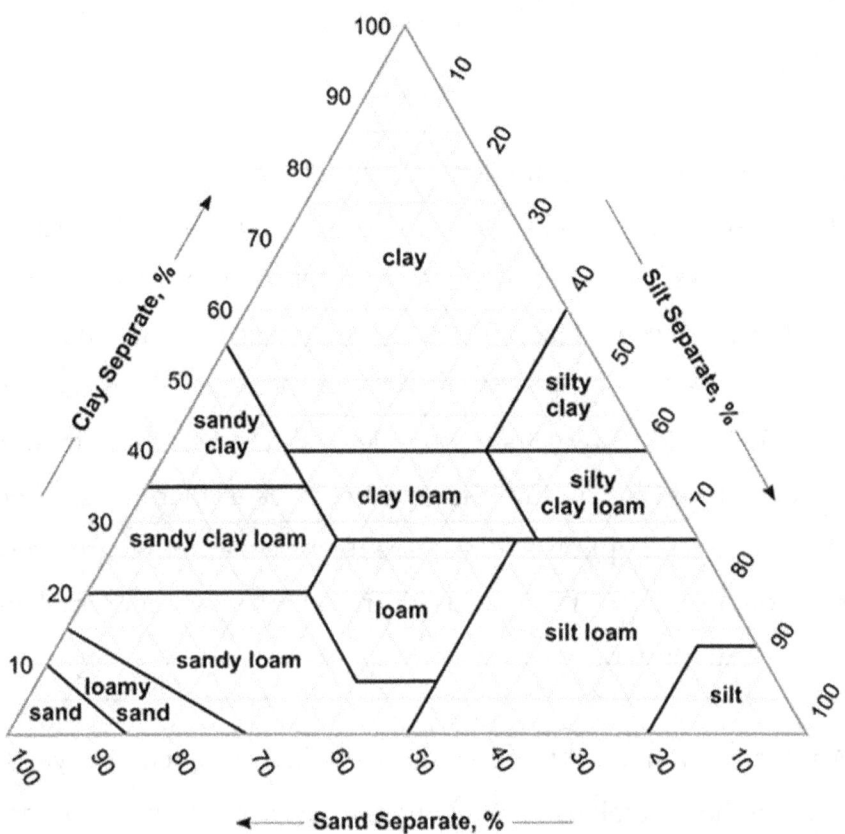

Protecting Your Garden

You aren't the only one who finds your garden attractive and welcoming! There's a host of critters and creatures that you will want to keep out of your garden, particularly a food garden. Fencing, strategic planting of strong-scented plants, herbs, and mulching are a few methods of protecting your garden from invasion. Other than the warm-blooded, winged, and legged kind, the other pests are weeds. They compete for resources, like little green bullies in the garden!

Weeds

Pulling out weeds the moment you spot them is quite effective. It stops them in their tracks before they set seed. However, mulching is a highly effective and inexpensive method of protecting your plants from weeds. The mulch acts as a physical barrier between the soil and light, inhibiting the germination of seeds. Use shredded bark, straw, or shredded leaves in two or three-inch (5-8 cm) thick layers to reduce the growth of weeds. Planting smother crops is also an option — these are dense cover crops grown on bare soil to crowd out the weeds. Do not allow smother crop plants to set seed, though!

Another option is utilizing landscape fabric to block out weeds. This method involves rolling out the fabric over your soil and cutting holes or slots where you want your plants to grow. It's a pretty simple and effective way to keep your garden weed-free, and is gaining popularity amongst the gardening community.

Garden Pests

More than likely your garden will be visited by pests in some shape or form. Below is a list of 6 practical, non-chemical, tried-

and-true ways to control or stop pests from wreaking havoc in your precious garden:

1. Garden fences provide a physical barrier around your garden to keep out deer, cats and dogs, rabbits, chickens, and other unwanted guests.
2. Burrowing pests such as moles, voles and gophers can destroy your garden from below the surface. Your raised bed should be enough to deterrent them, but if you find that a crafty pest has found its way into your garden, then burying a common garden barrier such as fabric or steel mesh should do the trick.
3. Mulching is an easy material to find and is effective in deterring many common garden pests. Rough mulch and sharp material like coarse gravel, shells, and stones can help deter larger animals as well.
4. Hanging noisy items around the garden can scare off animals, like tin cans or old pans, but do consider whether you (or your neighbors) are happy about the noise that follows every time a wind blows!
5. Planting thorny plants as a border can prevent entry into the garden such as slugs and snails. You could even build up a simple thornbush wall to keep larger animals from poking their noses into your garden.
6. Growing herbs or scented plants that the animals dislike is an effective way to keep many pests out of the garden. Check your local gardening center for advice on the best, most effective plants to use for your area.

3

CONTAINER GARDENING

Gardening Almost Anywhere

Barrels, bags, baskets, buckets, pots, and tubs — anything goes when it comes to container gardening! Pots offer versatility and flexibility in arrangement and can be hung, mounted, or placed on a pedestal if not on the ground. They serve as fabulous accents and focal points alike. This gardening method offers a multitude of possibilities, a method that presents the perfect opportunity for expressing creativity!

Why Container Gardening?

Container gardening offers the most versatility and convenience when compared to other forms of gardening. You can carry your plants around and rearrange them by season or preference as you please — no transplanting necessary! Also, it is a convenient way of growing fresh herbs, fruits, vegetables, and beautiful plants if all you have is a patio, balcony, or a small yard. You can use container gardening in a small section of your yard, as well, if you find a space that has good sunlight and potential! You can bring your fresh produce and herbs right to your kitchen window or to your doorstep with container gardening. For areas where the weather is unpredictable or harsh, container gardening offers you the option of quickly moving your plants to a safer space until bad weather passes.

Benefits of Container Gardening

The benefits of container gardening are many. Growing in containers offers you the opportunity to grow plants that have different nutrient, soil, or water requirements and have them arranged next to each other. It is an easier method of gardening for the elderly, children, or those with limited mobility. There's barely any room for weeds to take root in containers, resulting in far less weeding. Growing plants in separate pots prevent disease spread and makes it harder for insects to travel from plant to plant. You can play with your color scheme and pot arrangement as you please, making work in the garden fun and exciting. Invasive plants may be grown in pots without the fear of them taking over the entire garden! Furthermore, it's a great alternative for renters as your plants can move house with you!

Container Sizes

Different plants have different container size requirements. Determining the size of the container required for a plant is based on the plant's root system. The deeper the root system of a plant, the deeper and larger the container it has to be planted in. Container size is important because the pots you grow your plants have to be large enough for the mature plants to thrive. The container houses the soil and the moisture that the plant will need to produce leaves, flowers, and fruits. Containers also have to be large enough for the height and weight of the plant growing in it not to tip it over.

List of Container Sizes Depending on Plant

This chart[4] is a useful reference and source of information on container size recommendations for some common plants. It will also give you an idea of how much soil is needed and how many bags to buy if needed based on the container size used.

Plant	Light Needed	Min. Container Size * (metric)	Number of Plants** (metric)	Space Between Plants (metric)
Arugula	Full/part sun	1/2 gal (2 L)	3-5 plants	3-4 in (8-10 cm)
Bachelor Buttons	Full sun	1-2 qt (1-2 L)	3-5 plants	3-4 in (8-10 cm)
Beans, Bush	Full sun	2 gal (7.5 L)	3 plants	4-6 in (10-15 cm)
Beans, Pole	Full sun	5 gal (19 L)	3 plants	2-4 in (5-10 cm)
Basil	Full sun	1 qt (1 L)	1 plant	-
Broccoli	Full sun	5 gal (19 L)	1-2 plants	12-18 in (30-45 cm)
Calendula	Full sun	1-2 qt (1-2 L)	3-5 plants	3-4 in (8-10 cm)
Cantaloupe	Full sun	5 gal (19 L)	1 plant	-
Carrots	Full/part sun	1-5 gal (3.5-19 L)	8-10 per gal (3.5 L)	2-3 in (5-8 cm)
Cabbage	Full/part sun	5-15 gal (19-57 L)	1 per 5 gal (19 L)	12-18 in (30-45 cm)
Chard, Swiss	Full/part sun	1 gal (3.5 L)	4-5 plants	4-6 in (10-15 cm)
Chives	Full sun	1 qt (1 L)	3 plants	-
Cilantro	Full sun	1-5 gal (3.5-19 L)	1 per gal (3.5 L)	8-12 in (20-30 cm)
Collards	Full sun	1-5 gal (3.5-19 L)	3 per gal (3.5 L)	5-7 in (13-18 cm)
Cucumbers	Full sun	3-5 gal (11-19 L)	3 plants	Hill plants in the middle
Cucumbers, bush	Full sun	3-5 gal (11-19 L)	1 plant	-
Dianthus	Full sun	1-2 qt (1-2 L)	3-5 plants	3-4 in (8-10 cm)

Plant	Light Needed	Min. Container Size * (metric)	Number of Plants** (metric)	Space Between Plants (metric)
Dill	Full sun	1-5 gal (3.5-19 L)	10-12 per gal (3.5 L)	8-12 in (20-30 cm)
Eggplant	Full sun	2-5 gal (7.5-19 L)	3 plants	-
Hyssop	Full sun	0.5-1 gal (2-4 L)	1 plant	-
Kale	Full/part sun	2-5 gal (7.5-19 L)	3 plants	10-15 in (25-38 cm)
Lettuce, leaf	Full/part sun	0.5-5 gal (2-19 L)	10-12 per gal (3.5 L)	2-3 in (5-8 cm)
Marigold	Full sun	1-2 qt (1-2 L)	3-5 plants	3-4 in (8-10 cm)
Nasturtium	Full/part sun	1-2 qt (1-2 L)	3-5 plants	3-4 in (8-10 cm)
Onions	Full/part sun	2-5 gal (7.5-19 L)	3-5 mature plants	Thin to 4-5 in (10-13 cm)
Onions, green	Full/part sun	1 gal (1 L)	10-12 plants	2-3 in (5-8 cm)
Oregano	Full sun	1 gal (1 L)	1 plant	-
Pansy	Part shade	1-2 qt (1-2 L)	3-6 plants	3-4 in (8-10 cm)
Parsley	Full/part sun	1-2 qt (1-2 L)	1 plant	-
Peas	Full/part sun	2-5 gal (7.5-19 L)	3-6 plant	3-4 in (8-10 cm)
Peas, snow	Full/part sun	2-5 gal (7.5-19 L)	3-6 plants	3-4 in (8-10 cm)
Peppers, bell	Full sun	2-5 gal (7.5-19 L)	1 plant	-
Peppers, hot	Full sun	2-5 gal (7.5-19 L)	1 plant	-
Pepper, wax	Full sun	2-5 gal (7.5-19 L)	1 plant	-
Pumpkin	Full sun	1 gal (1 L)	1 plant	-
Radicchio	Full/part sun	1 gal (1 L)	3 plants	-

Plant	Light Needed	Min. Container Size * (metric)	Number of Plants** (metric)	Space Between Plants (metric)
Sage	Full sun	1 gal (1 L)	1 plant	-
Spearmint	Full/part sun	1-2 qt (1-2 L)	3-5 plants	3-4 in (8-10 cm)
Squash	Full sun	5 gal (19 L)	1 plant	-
Squash, summer	Full sun	5 gal (19 L)	1 plant	-
Thyme	Full sun	1-2 qt (1-2 L)	1 plant	-
Tomato	Full sun	5 gal (19 L)	1 plant	-
Tomato, cherry	Full sun	2 gal (7.5 L)	1 plant	-
Watermelon, sugar	Full sun	5 gal (19 L)	1 plant	-
Zucchini	Full sun	5 gal (19 L)	1 plant	-

*Smaller containers need watering more frequently.

**Depending on the shape of the container, it is better to consider the spacing.

Container Drainage

While you can certainly use practically anything as a planter, the single most important thing to take care of before making it a plant's home is drainage. This is as simple as drilling a few holes into the container so that any excess water has a means of exiting the container when the soil is saturated.

Why Drainage is Critical

Of the many factors that lend themselves to the health of your container plant, drainage is the most critical — it spells the life and death of your leafy friend! Without proper drainage, excess water accumulates in the bottom of the container, presenting the risk of root rot and drowning your plant. Contrary to popular belief, more plants die as a result of excess water than are killed by a lack of water. Always remember – the more drainage your container has, the better for your plant!

Prevent Soil from Escaping Through Drainage Holes

After potting your plant and getting the soil just right, the last thing you want is for it to run out of the pot through the drainage holes! Lay a porous material at the bottom of the pot to allow water to pass while still containing your soil. Ensure that you don't use a material that will disintegrate over time with moisture. Netted material, fabric, and window screen are all examples of what you may use. An added advantage of covering drainage holes is that your containers will be protected from naughty insects that may want to crawl into the pot! It is worth noting here that while it is common for a layer of stones, gravel, rocks, or similar to be added at the bottom of containers, this should be avoided as they can lead to root rot and possibly impede drainage.

Lift Containers Off the Ground

When you've gone through the trouble of mixing a well-draining soil, lining your pot for drainage, and positioning the drainage holes, the least you can do is lift the container off of the ground so that the holes aren't blocked by the surface the pot is resting on. Elevating pots is as simple as adding feet to them or placing pots on a planter caddy. Anything goes — let your creativity flow!

Container Soil

Container gardening requires that you pay a little more attention to your soil. Unfortunately, the soil from the yard or garden bed is far too dense for container growing and may contain unwanted bugs, weed seeds, or other diseases. No matter how happy your ground-growing plants may be, never use the soil as-is from a garden bed for container gardening exclusively.

Fundamentals of Potting Soil

Containers require a lighter mix to offer the best environment for growth. It is usually a mix of materials like husks, mosses, barks, and volcanic rock particles, producing a perfect medium for offering good drainage, air circulation, and moisture retention. Perlite and vermiculite are used to improve drainage, prevent compacted soil and increase moisture retention with an added bonus that they wont disintegrate over time. Sphagnum moss, peat moss, and coir are added to the potting mix for their water retention abilities. Compost can be added to the soil mix to introduce nutrients. To bulk it up and stretch it further, clean garden soil may be added to the container soil mix to about 20% volume. When adding garden soil to your container soil mix, ensure that you do not use soil contaminated by disease or pests. Garden soil can be baked to sterilize before mixing if preferred.

Custom recipes for homemade potting soil and soilless mix

Commercially mixed potting soils are formulated to meet all the criteria necessary for healthy plant growth, but it comes at a high price. Not only is preparing your own soil mix far more economical, but it is also an opportunity to prepare custom mixes as required for different applications. Finer mixtures are preferred for seed starter containers, while potted shrubs and trees benefit from a higher percentage of coarse material than typical tropical and fruiting plants. Cactus and succulents are happier in gravelly and sandy soils, which aren't appreciated by other plants. Preparing your own media gives you control over the formulation and is easier to do than purchasing and storing several different types of soils.

Media Ingredients

The following is a basic recipe for soil-based potting media[5]. In this recipe, garden loam soil, coarse construction sand, and sphagnum peat moss are combined in equal parts by volume: Soil-based or peat-based potting media can be made at home by combining individual ingredients.

- Sphagnum peat moss has a coarse texture and contributes to good aeration yet provides water holding capacity to prevent soil from drying too quickly. Adding too much sphagnum peat, however, can restrict soil drainage by holding too much water. Sphagnum peat moss can be difficult to wet and should be moistened before mixing in other ingredients. Alternatives to peat moss can be coconut coir, leaf/wood mulch, biochar, or rice hulls. Use accordingly as these alternatives hold their own unique properties compared with peat moss and may need to be mixed with another ingredient (i.e., compost) to achieve similar results.
- Coarse, sharp, or builder sand, often used in construction, is a primary ingredient in potting media. Like peat moss, sand improves drainage and aeration but does not improve water-holding capacity. Too much sand will make containers too heavy to move. Sand should not be mixed with clay-based soil.
- Perlite can be used in both peat-based and soil-based potting media in place of sand. Perlite is an expanded volcanic rock (fluoride-based) manufactured when heated to 1,800°F (982°C). Like sand, perlite provides excellent drainage but is lighter in weight and holds more air.

Although more expensive than sand, the advantages may outweigh the additional cost. Disadvantages of perlite include; 1) a tendency to float to the top of the medium when watered; 2) an inability to hold or retain water; and 3) a need to be moistened before it is mixed into other ingredients to reduce dust, which is harmful if inhaled.

- Vermiculite is often used instead of perlite. Vermiculite is clay belonging to the mica family and is naturally found in laminated flakes. It expands when folds of vermiculite can hold water, nutrients, and air, unlike perlite. Only horticultural grades, sold at garden centers, are recommended. Vermiculite can easily compact, which reduces its ability to hold water and air.

Homemade <u>Soil-based</u> Potting Media Recipe

1. Start with 1 gallon (4 L) of **sterilized loam soil**, commonly called garden soil and sold at garden centers, and pour it into a clean, empty bushel basket (35 L). Sterilized loam soil is worth the cost to avoid disease, insect, and weed problems that may exist in unsterilized soil. Soil taken directly from the garden may be contaminated with these pests, causing future problems such as dead, deformed, or stunted seedlings. Weeds in garden soil generally grow vigorously and crowd out desired seedlings by competing for nutrients, water, air, and light.

2. Add 1 gallon (4 L) of moist, coarse **sphagnum peat moss**, followed by one gallon of coarse sand, perlite, or vermiculite.
3. Adjust the texture of the medium to create a loose, well-drained mixture. Sand feels gritty, and clay feels sticky. If the potting soil feels too sandy, more peat moss should be added. If the potting soil feels too sticky, extra sand and peat moss should be added. Adjust the texture by adding small portions of sand or peat moss until you are satisfied with the texture.

Homemade Soilless Potting Media Recipe

Soilless mixes or peat-based potting media do not contain any soil but generally consist of peat moss combined with horticultural grades of vermiculite or perlite and added fertilizer. Peat-based media are helpful for seed germination because they are relatively sterile, light in texture and weight, and uniform. The light texture enables seeds to readily germinate and emerge, allows tender roots to grow, and makes transplanting seedlings easier.

In general, standard media recipes are created based on the plants being grown (e.g., bedding plants, potted plants, or seed germination). A standard recipe for a homemade soilless mix consists of half sphagnum peat moss and half perlite or vermiculite. To mix ½ bushel (18 L) basket or 4 gallons (15 L) of media:

1. Start by pouring 2 gallons (7.5 L) of peat moss into the bushel basket.
2. Add 2 gallons (7.5 L) of either perlite or vermiculite and mix thoroughly.
3. Moisten the mix before using it in pots or flats.

Container Materials

Another exciting aspect of container gardening is that there are so many different types of containers to choose from. With respect to material choice, you have to consider maintenance, cost, aesthetic appeal, porosity, weight, and location in addition to size, color, and shape.

Terracotta

These pots are made from baked clay. They are the typical pot that would spring to mind if you were asked to think of a potted plant. Terracotta planters and pots are porous, allowing water and air to pass freely through the container walls, lowering the risk of overwatering. On the other hand, this does mean that plants in terracotta pots dry out faster than many other pot materials. These are heavy pots, well suited for larger plants. Terracotta pots age and wear with water and mineral deposits and are prone to cracking in cold weather.

Ceramic Glazed

These containers are the best of the clay and plastic worlds. Ceramic glazed pots are clay pots with a nonporous glaze. These glazed pots retain moisture longer than terracotta, lending themselves well to those who may underwater their plants. They are heavy and more durable than terracotta in harsh weather. Unfortunately, the non-porous glaze does inhibit airflow and can be a poor choice for people concerned about overwatering. They are fragile and likely to crack if dropped.

Plastic

Plastic is non-porous, so if you happen to be a chronic underwaterer, they will retain moisture for your plant. For the same reason, over-waterers, beware! Lack of porosity also inhibits airflow through the medium. However, these pots are lighter, more durable, and come in a wider variety of sizes, shapes, and designs. Of course, plastic is not the choice for the eco-conscious gardener. Milk crates are another option as they can be repurposed to make great portable planters. Think about it — crates are made for people to carry them around — they're perfect little planters. The crate simply needs to be lined with a porous material and filled with soil, and you're good to go!

Fabric

Fabric grow bags are a popular option these days as they are relatively cheap to buy and highly effective for growing beautiful plants! They are typically made from a thick breathable fabric, similar to a burlap or reusable grocery bag. Grow-bags are breathable, and drainage is much better than traditional plastic pots. Choose a grow bag that is of good quality and reusable.

Wood

The natural charm of wood is a tough aesthetic to beat in the garden. Wood has the added advantage of insulating plant roots in cold weather. Stains and sealers should be avoided as they can introduce toxins to your soils. Using plastic liners enhances the lifespan of wooden planters, but treated and waterproofed, dense wooden planters are generally rather durable. Unlined and untreated wooden planters will rot with time. Unfortunately, pests like carpenter ants and sow bugs will love your wooden planters as much or more than you do, burrowing into them and taking residence within their walls.

Cement

Durability is by far the strongest advantage of a cement planter. Cement pots are long-lasting and environmentally friendly, withstanding the toughest weather and wear and tear. The lighter color of cement prevents overheating of the plant roots in hot weather, while the density of its walls offers insulation for the roots in cold weather. Cement planters trump size and volume, perfect for statement pieces or large shrubs, trees, or bushes. Of course, they are incredibly heavy relative to their size and can prove difficult to lug around. They are also prone to cracking when the weather falls to below-freezing temperatures.

Container Preparation

Preparing containers for your plants is an important task. The container will serve as your plant's home, and you want to get it just right for them to thrive. The good news is that preparing pots is simple! As with many things regarding gardening, the task at hand is easy; you just have to wrap your head around the basics!

How to prepare pots and containers for gardening

First things first, if you are using a layer of fabric or net-like material to cover the drainage holes, lay down the material over the bottom of the pot, doubling the material if necessary. Don't fill a layer of rock, Styrofoam, broken materials, or anything of the sort at the bottom of your pot! Simply lay down the fabric and begin filling your container with potting soil mixture. If you are filling a very large pot and it will be heavy to move once filled, position it and then fill it on the spot. Next, completely saturate the potting soil with water, using a steady stream of water instead of a harsh squirt. Water several times if necessary. Using warm or tepid water will help the soil absorb water more easily. Allow the soil to drain and settle. That's it! You're ready to tuck in some plants or seeds, as you wish!

Choosing Plants for Containers

With so many plants to choose from, it's only natural to feel overwhelmed! Here you find out which are the best plants to start with — the ones that are pot-friendly!

Pro Tip: Sometimes, the simplest way to decide what you'd like to have in your containers is to poke around on the internet for ideas. Sites like Pinterest or YouTube will likely give you some amazing ideas for easy container plants you could try.

Vegetables and herbs

While it is true that almost anything can be grown in a container, there are still some plants that are far easier than others when it comes to container gardening. Here we take a brief look at the best container plants for an easy garden, for the beginner, or the gardener looking for low maintenance.

First, on the list, we have nightshade vegetables — juicy **tomatoes**, majestic **eggplant**, proud **peppers** (both hot and sweet), and even the humble **potato**. Fast-growing crops like **peas**, **radish**, and **lettuce** also do well in containers. Another easy-growing vegetable is **squash**, a beautiful container plant with so many varieties to select from! If you like the idea of a plant tumbling out of the pot, **cucumbers** are container-friendly, too. **Strawberries** are very pot-friendly, as are **blueberries** and small **melons**. When it comes to herbs, any herb performs well in a container. The easiest and most popular to grow are **basil, rosemary, oregano, thyme, lemon balm**, and **mint**.

Annuals

The perfect plant for a pot that doesn't need pampering? We have a few. Cascading **verbena** makes for a beautiful sight — clusters of bright blooms that don't need any fussing over! For visual impact, nothing beats the simplicity and aesthetic of a few **sweet potato** varieties grown in a pot, with their magnificent green vines trailing out of the pit and over the ground. For fun foliage, plant **coleus** — a sun-loving plant that can be kept safe from frost by moving indoors until the frost has passed. The red, pink, purple, and green leaves are quite a sight! **Scaevola** is another low-maintenance plant that is a dream to grow in a container; the plant produces masses of blue flowers that don't even require deadheading! This plant will happily grow in any sunny spot, attracting beautiful butterflies to your space.

Perennials and shrubs

Looking for a permanent resident for your pots? These perennials and shrubs can lie for years in containers — no need for digging up, discarding, propagating, or repotting every year. One of the toughest container plants in this category is the **"Golden Sword" yucca**, which you can grow alongside most other plants for a colorful pot year-round. **"Green Mountain" boxwood** is a plant that remains a deep, dark green all year. A slow-growing shrub, its growth will be stunted somewhat in a container but stunning nonetheless. For a cascading creeper, look no further than the **Golden creeping Jenny**, which loves plenty of water and a warm sunny spot. For height, the **"Emerald" arborvitae** is easy to care for, tolerant of both sun and shade, and year-round visual interest. Another classic container favorite is the glossy, shiny **bergenia**, which often performs even better in containers than they do in beds! Finally, the list wouldn't be complete without a winter flowering plant — enter the **Japanese Pieris**. It boasts evergreen foliage and striking blossoms that carry an intoxicating scent in spring and a rich color in winter.

Container Gardening Care

Your container garden has the potential to thrive even better than a traditional bed-type garden — thanks to the individual care each plant can receive. However, with your plant growing in pots rather than in plots, a couple of factors need close attention for container garden success. Here we take a look at five easy steps to follow in caring for a successful container garden.

5 Steps for Container Gardening Maintenance

These are the five steps you need to take care of your container garden and keep it flourishing.

1. Water frequently

Once your plants are placed in containers, they are more prone to drying out. The smaller the volume of soil held by the container, the faster it will dry out. Take special care to keep container soil moist at all times, sometimes watering as frequently as twice a day in the summer heat. Ensure that you do not simply dampen the surface of the soil — saturate the pot completely. If you notice the soil drying out far too quickly, there may be too many plants in that volume of soil. Either remove some plants, prune some back or move the container into a shady spot.

2. Fertilize regularly

You need to feed your plants! This is especially true for fruits and vegetables. They get hungry, requiring a consistent supply of nutrients to grow their best stems, stalks, leaves, and fruits. The limited volume of soil your plants are growing in makes fertilizing critical. Potting soil typically doesn't come with many nutrients to keep your plants healthy for longer than two or three weeks. When transplanting plants to pots, be sure to work slow-release fertilizer into the soil before planting. Feeding your plant with additional nutrients is as easy as offering a drink of compost tea, seaweed emulsion, or liquid fertilizer every two weeks or as needed. Use a weak dilution of either a half or a quarter strength if watering every week.

3. Groom and remove dead flowers

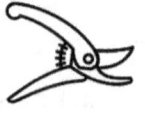
We all want lush, full plants filling our containers. You can achieve this by pruning down any leggy stems, removing damaged or diseased foliage, and picking off the spent blooms before seeds begin to set. These simple tricks encourage a healthier plant and make sure your plant is always looking its best.

4. Change plants seasonally

Like all living things, plants get old. They begin to look tired and worn once they have lived past their prime, at which point you should consider digging them up and either replacing them with a new, fresh plant of the same kind or follow the seasons and always have a different plant to look at. The spring container garden brims with green foliage and new growth, promising great things to come. The summer garden is a rich display of color, fruits, and berries — think of a window basket full of strawberries and herbs or potted fruit trees flanking your home entrance. The autumn garden is a dramatic turn of color, a time for beautiful kales and leafy vegetables towering in shallow pots and fat pumpkins tumbling out of heavy containers. Winter can be a warm affair if you plant winter-flowering shrubs or fruiting citruses and beautiful vines that don't get bitten by the frost.

5. Prepare for winter (winterizing)

Understanding your climate zone is critical for a rewarding garden experience. If you live in a cold climate, your containers need protection from dipping temperatures since the small volumes of soil are less insulating for plants' roots than the ground. Beware of keeping terracotta and ceramic containers outdoors in freezing conditions, as they may crack. Empty these pots and store them until the weather warms up. For containers with permanent residents, heavily mulch them and store them in a sheltered space, preferably a garage, basement, or sealed balcony or sunroom.

10 Steps to Building Your Container Garden

You are ten steps away from your very own beautiful container garden! Simply follow these steps and work your way closer to a new and exciting outdoor space.

1. The Container

Picking a pot is fun — so many colors, styles, shapes, and sizes to choose from. Wherever possible, pick the largest container you can for your plants. The larger the container, the more soil it can hold, and the more soil it can hold, the more room for your plant's roots to grow into! Drainage holes are extremely important, so, if necessary, drill extra holes into the pot as needed.

2. The Container Prep

Using oversized containers certainly does make for an attractive focal point in the garden. Of course, when you see a gigantic pot, the first thing you worry about is how you will move it around or how you will fill it with an expensive growth medium. Here's the trick: fill up the container with light, durable and non-compactable materials until you have the amount of space you want to fill with soil or potting mix. You can fill the bottom of the pot with other pots, purchasable inserts, large rocks, or even broken ceramic. The idea is to fill up the volume so that you don't need to use as much potting mix. Just remember to keep the drainage holes free as I mentioned above.

3. The Soil

Fill the container with the soil of your choice until a few inches (7 cm or so) from the rim of the container. Do not mound the soil. After some time and a few waterings, you may need to add a little more potting mix to the container since the mixture will compact and settle over time.

4. The Food

While not essential, starter food is an excellent addition to your container to help your plants get a good healthy start. Starter food encourages plants to grow strong root systems, which leads to healthier foliage and fruit setting, longer-lasting blooms, and better color throughout the plant. Also, when transplanting, using starter food minimizes the risk of plant loss do to shock.

5. The Plants

When choosing plants to grow in containers, select the kinds that have the same water, nutrition, and light requirements. For example, growing cacti with pansies will be disappointing, as will growing nitrogen-fixing beans with fruiting vegetable plants that prefer more phosphorus rather than nitrogen.

6. The Plant Prep

When transplanting your plants, groom them first. Remove drying or yellowing leaves, spent blooms, or rotting areas. Loosen the roots and carefully cut root-bound root systems. Prune back leggy plants down to the leaf node on branches. Pinch off blooms in flowering plants when transplanting to encourage the plant to take in its new home before setting flowers again.

7. The Planting

While containers can look fabulous with a single statement plant, there's also a lot to be said about a container full of variety. When planting several kinds of plants in a single container, place the tallest plants at the center of the pot and surround this with filler plants until tumbling, trailing varieties are placed at the edges. Make sure that you do not compress the soil too much when planning to allow the roots to get airflow.

8. The Watering

Your plants are thirsty after all the hard work — yes, your work, but nonetheless, they need a drink! Saturate the soil slowly and steadily with a gentle stream of water from a hose or watering can until the water seeps out of the drainage holes. If the medium is exceptionally dry, a few waterings will have to be done to saturate it completely.

9. The Fertilizing

The sure-fire way to healthy plants in containers — other than maintaining hydration — is to feed them with phosphate fertilizer. Phosphate encourages strong root systems and results in plants with bigger, better, and more colorful blooms and better fruit settings. Phosphates benefit ornamentals, vegetables, orchids, flowering shrubs, berry bushes, and container plants alike.

10. The Maintenance

With all the effort you have put into getting your plants off to a good start, don't let it all go to waste by neglecting them through the season! Keep an eye out for disease, trim branches as needed, deadhead flowers, cut back plants so that they maintain their form and shape, pluck out any pesky weeds if they find their way into your pots, and ensure that you say a kind word or two to your little green friend — they like compliments just as much as we do!

Pro tip: As plants lose their bloom, pinch or cut off the flower stem below the spent flower instead of just plucking the dead flower off.

Sample Container Project Ideas

- Containers don't always need to be the traditional vessel. Get creative and convert almost anything into a garden display! For example, a set of shutters can be hung against a wall, with its slots filled up with enough soil to house an attractive assortment of succulents.
- Who of us doesn't have a shoe hanger?! Whether it's an old functional hanger that you've grown tired of or a tattered one that doesn't serve its purpose anymore, you can absolutely use a shoe organizer as a garden arrangement! Fill a little potting mix in each pocket and some easy-growing, shallow-rooted succulents who won't mind when the soil dries out!
- Create a cozy outdoor space by grouping large containers and planters, brimming with healthy foliage and colorful blooms. Make a great spot for tea, for diving into a book, or simply for a few minutes of peace and silence!
- Transform a regular birdbath into a zen garden piece with a few well-placed succulents and some pebbles. Plant a few tumbling varieties near the edges for some drama.
- Climbers are a small space's friend. They draw attention upwards, with long tendrils, branches, or vines that attract the eye. A bougainvillea makes for a great patio plant, where it can reach out from its pot to the tippy-top of your fencing or your boundary walls.

- Decorate an outdoor staircase with pots of interestingly shaped foliage and blooms placed on the ends of each stair for a vibrant walkway.
- Use oversized jumbo planters with shrubs and small trees to offer privacy in the garden in a grand and gloriously green way!
- Create visual interest with not only variation in plants, but pots too. A group of mismatched pots of varying heights, patterns, and colors can be a point of interest in an otherwise forgotten corner or neglected space in the yard.
- Use old steel or a wooden table to display an assortment of herbs, posing in their pots and simply begging to be snipped and added to your soups!

Balcony flower boxes filled with beautiful plants.

4

RAISED BED GARDENING

The Green Thumb Advantage

Even the greenest thumb can't perform miracles when plants are grown in poor soil. There's simply no way around it, for the lush leaves you love, you have to grow your plants in soil rich in organic matter and brimming with good bugs to aerate the soil and make more nutrients available for your leafy friends. Raised beds are the solution for almost any soil problem, whether it's poor nutrient content, contamination, or bad composition. A raised bed gives the gardener control over the soil, allowing for the perfect growing medium for their plants. It also provides options for attaching accessories such as lids or "hoops" to create a mini-greenhouse, as well as overhead structures to provide shade or irrigation options.

What are Raised Beds

Raised beds can simply be thought of as large, immovable planters. They are mounds of soil typically encased in a frame, supported by the ground. A raised bed only requires a frame made from a material of your choice and then filled with the soil of your choice. They can range in height, width and depth, according to your specific wants and needs.

Advantages of Raised Beds

Raised Bed Gardening is a gardening technique that offers many benefits. It is a method of gardening that provides an easy solution to several gardeners' problems.

1. Control Over Health of the Soil

Raised beds place complete control of the soil quality in your hands. You can fill your raised garden bed with whatever nutrients and soil type your plants will need. Of course, having a plan for what you intend to plant in the bed will affect your soil choices. With raised bed gardening, you can have a bed of acid-loving plants thriving next to a bed of plants loving their alkaline soil! Since your soil is in raised containers, the soil won't be tread on and compacted, and it will be protected from runoff from heavy rains.

2. Puts Plants at Eye Level for Better Detection of Pest Issues

When your plants are growing in the ground, it can be difficult to spot disease and pests until it's too late. With your plants closer to your nose, they'll be closer to your eyes so you can spot the small signs of infestation and attack before it's too late. The fact that inspecting your plants will be less of an effort will have you doing it more often, increasing the chances of catching bugs before they win the battle against your plants!

3. Added Convenience of Not Having to Bend Down

You never quite realize just how much work you'll be doing on your knees when you take up gardening until you do it. Traditional in-garden beds have you kneeling on all fours, inspecting your plants' leaves, plucking out weeds and planting, tilling, and fertilizing. A raised garden bed brings your plants up to you — that little less of a journey to reach them sure makes all the difference on your knees and back in the long run! You can make your raised bed in such a way that you have easy access to every plant from the sides.

4. Taller Beds are Great for Elderly or Disabled People

While raised beds are typically only about a foot (30 cm) high off the ground, they can be raised as high as you prefer. This makes eye-level gardening a real possibility, allowing for the disabled, mobility challenged, and the elderly to enjoy gardening and growing plants without strain on their joints, back, or knees. Simply put, raised beds have the potential to make gardening comfortable!

5. Prevents Plant Roots from Reaching Contaminants That Might Naturally Occur

As much as you would like to, there's no way to control everything. In gardening, your environment plays a large role in your garden and its success. While we cannot control every environmental factor, the good news is that gardeners have many methods and tools to mitigate the effects brought on by the environment. Surprising as it may seem, soil contamination can occur naturally. This can happen through any means, like the natural presence of arsenic or rainwater bringing in chemical contaminants. Raised beds keep your plants out of reach and safe from these and other factors.

Things to Consider Before Using Raised Beds

 As simple as raised beds are to make, it requires more than a mound of soil contained just anywhere in the garden. Here are a couple of things to think over to get the perfect placement of your beds and improve your crops!

Sunlight

We've already touched on the importance of sunlight when it comes to healthy plant growth and development, so it goes without saying that you have to plan your raised garden beds in areas that have the best access to light as possible. If you can increase sunlight by selectively pruning trees or moving structures obstructing the light, then do so — your plants will thank you!

Leveling of the Terrain

You can place a raised bed over a terrain of any kind. However, try to level out the area you plan to build your raised bed on, as this will simplify the preparation of the bed. If, for whatever reason, you cannot level out the land, make sure that the finished raised bed is level on the surface. Simply take the uneven ground into account when building your raised bed.

Access to Water

Suppose there is no source of water nearby. In that case, you may consider laying a soaker hose or other form of irrigation into the beds. Alternatively, you could bring a faucet closer to the beds, but do consider the costs of the plumbing versus the hose irrigation. If you plan on using a long hose to water the beds, consider the convenience of reeling it up daily. Rain barrels or containers are popular for most gardeners. These can be placed at a downspout to capture the rain runoff from the roof or standalone and filled periodically with a garden house from the nearest water source.

Proximity to Your Home

The closer your garden is to your home, the more likely you spend more time in it. Simply walking through the garden while you sip on your tea, appreciating your plants and the garden you've built, is a rewarding experience. However, you also want your herbs and fresh produce close by so that you're only a few steps away from fresh food when you're cooking away at the stovetop. So, don't pick a spot that's far from the house, as it will be not only inconvenient but also impractical.

Environmental Conditions

Consider the environmental conditions that may affect your raised beds in the specific area you have chosen for their placement. Will water be pooling in that area, increasing the likelihood of flooding your beds? Will runoff direct to that area contaminate your beds over time?

Potential Predators in the Area

If your outdoor space happens to be a popular meet-up spot for furry and feathered creatures, you may want to consider fencing your raised beds for added protection. Hoop houses are also an option. Bendable PVC conduit from the hardware store is often used to create "half hoops" over your raised bed. Simply cover the hoops with bird netting or landscape shade cloth to keep animals out. The closer your garden beds are to your home, the less likely wildlife will interfere in your garden!

Raised Bed Sizes

Raised beds come in all shapes and sizes. You are free to choose the dimensions and materials for your raised bed, but be sure to consider the practicality of your choices. Here I offer a few guidelines to follow for the most practical shape and size for a raised garden bed.

Height

The typical range for raised beds is between 12 and 18 inches (30-45 cm), but going as high up as 36 inches (76 cm). The height of your garden bed is largely dependent on the quality of the soil beneath it and on the kind of plants you intend to grow in the bed. Naturally, the poorer the soil quality beneath the bed, the higher you want to raise the bed to give your plants more quality soil to grow in. Shallow raised beds are practical for shallow-rooted plants, like lettuce and some spinach. Also, if you are fortunate enough to have quality soil that you are building over, you don't have to raise your bed as high. Bear in mind that the taller the bed, the more support it will require to maintain its shape and sturdiness. Once you plan for a bed with sides higher than 18 inches (45 cm), it is best to factor in support boards in the structure to account for the mass of the soil it will hold.

Length

When it comes to length, it is simply whatever you fancy! Raised beds can be as long or as short as you prefer or as your space allows. Mixing up an arrangement of beds of different lengths makes for an interesting aesthetic. However, supports are, again, important. Cross supports need to be installed at a minimum of every 6 feet (183 cm) to secure the structural integrity of your raised bed. Your plants won't appreciate tumbling out of their beds! Lengthening your raised bed is a great way to maximize the space that you have available.

Width

Usually, the magic number is four feet (1.2 meters), but three feet (0.9 meters) is manageable as well. Four feet is great for spacing out plants well. However, beyond four feet wide means you'll be extending your arms to reach the center of your bed, which defeats the advantage of accessibility. So unless you have apishly long arms, four feet and under should do just fine.

Wall Thickness

Of course, the thickness of the walls of the raised bed you erect will depend on the material used to construct the actual bed. When measuring the lengths and widths of material required, don't neglect to take into account the thickness of the material. Note that the thinner the walls of the bed, the more critical the need for supports.

Spacing

The spacing between your raised beds is more important than you think. Not only do you need sufficient room for you to be able to walk between the raised beds comfortably, but you also need to have enough room to crouch down to get working in the beds with your tools on your knees. Having ample room for maneuvering your wheelbarrow between the raised beds makes weeding and cleaning up more convenient. On days when you don't feel like fighting with the weeds, you'll appreciate the space and convenience! Also, bear in mind that if you intend to grow grass between planters, you will need enough room for your lawnmower to fit through.

Raised Bed Materials

There is a wide variety of materials that you can build your garden beds from. If you're really wild, with lots of space and a good sense of humor, you could do one of each! Now that would make for quite a sight!

Standard Lumber

A clever way to minimize waste when building your raised beds from lumber is to consider the sizes that the lumber comes available in. Since common sizes available are 8, 10, and 12-foot lengths (2.4, 3, and 3.6 meters, respectively), maintaining your dimensions in multiples of 2 or 3 feet (0.6 or 0.9m) brings waste to a minimum. Choose lumber that is better suited to the outdoors in your region. Some popular choices are Cedar, Douglas Fir, Redwood, or Black Locust. Modern pressure-treated (PT) lumber techniques use safer treatments such as ACQ (Alkaline Copper Quaternary) than in the past. Avoid CCA (Chromated copper arsenate) treated lumber which has been discontinued since approximately 2003-2004 in many countries[6]. Ask your garden center or building supply store for more information on what wood products best suit your raised bed. Also, avoid applying any sort of paint or sealant to the wood unless it is an approved food-safe product.

Recycled Materials

Using recycled materials? Good on you! Do note that you will be restricted by the length of the material that you have. You have to work with the lengths to determine the dimensions of garden beds that will keep waste to a minimum.

Pro tip: Consider the "Shou Sugi Ban" wood preserving method. An ancient Japanese surface prepping technique that preserves wood by charring it with a flame. This not only gives the wood a beautiful black or black/brown finish, but it also helps protect the wood from the elements as well as deter bugs!

Concrete

Concrete is a trendy material growing in popularity for its flexibility, versatility, and durability. Yes, it is expensive, but if you are willing to invest in something that has a practically indefinite lifespan, then it may as well be concrete that can be molded to size and patterned as desired. Concrete is a material that can fit any style from farmhouse to contemporary and all the in-betweens.

Masonry

Masonry-raised beds are right at home in the garden! They make your raised beds appear almost seamless, blending in with the sand and rock. Masonry beds are a project from a skilled DIYer, but an unseasoned gardener may prefer to hire the pros on this one. The downside to this beautiful bed material is that it is permanent.

Cinder Block

Cinder Blocks are rather flexible when it comes to building raised garden beds. They may be arranged by simply stacking to form a bed or fixed with mortar for a permanent garden fixture. Achieving an elegant finish to your inexpensive cinder block beds comes at an uncharacteristically hefty price with capped tops and a stunning surface finish, but if you're gardening for aesthetics, then this is an idea to venture into.

Rock

Using boulders and cobbles to construct a raised bed allows you not only to shape your bed as desired but also to build a raised bed without the permanency of mortar, enabling you to shuffle the rocks around for a different bed as you please, when you please. If you have rocks on your property already, then your materials are free! But even if you don't, you can easily purchase rocks per volume.

Galvanized Culvert

These are large pipes typically used for roadway drainage, but when sliced into smaller sections, they make for excellent raised beds in a contemporary-look garden! Of course, culverts are stocked by building supply stores, but they are also sometimes available for free online when being disposed of. This is a no-fuss, no-assembly raised bed that holds plenty of potential for happy plants.

Stock Tanks

Quite easily one of the most effortless options when it comes to raised garden beds. Stock tanks are simply large troughs that are made for feeding animals but happen to be great for growing plants in! The only effort is in drilling in the drainage holes and then filling them up with dirt. These are stocked at farm stores and are inexpensive for their convenience. They are movable, sturdy, require no assembly, and are available in many sizes — what more could you ask for?

Steel

While there's plenty to love about using rock and wood and all things natural in a garden, there's something to be said about balancing the natural with the industrial. Using steel for making raised beds can add visual interest and a rustic element to your landscape. Steel sheets come in varying thicknesses and dimensions. They offer good sturdiness with a thin frame — hard to beat! The weathering of the steel sheets over time adds character to your garden, too! Steel roofing (sheeting) is an excellent option and usually comes with a galvanized coating which should prevent corrosion for years to come.

Constructing a Raised Bed

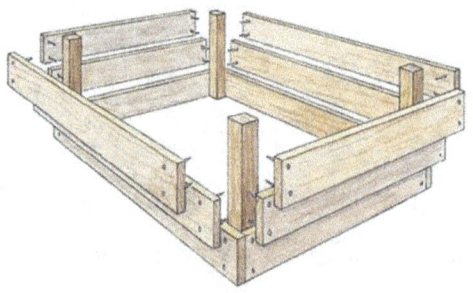

This is a barebones, no-fuss set of instructions to follow to build your raised garden beds so that you can get started with growing all those lovely plants you've got your eye on!

1. Choose a material to make your beds from.
2. Source the material; either buy new or recycle, but get your hands on all the material you need!
4. Pick a spot. Choose where you would like your bed to sit, and don't forget to consider the trees or structures nearby, the path of the sun, and proximity to water.
5. Build the frame of the bed. This is simply putting together the material to form the shape and size you desire. Fasten the bed frame and ensure that it is solid and sturdy. If necessary,

support the frame with the anchors or fasteners appropriate for the chosen material.

6. Lay a piece of landscaping fabric on the ground on the spot you have chosen to build your raised bed. Ensure that you cut the fabric a little oversized, enough for the frame to sit comfortably on the fabric to protect the frame. Use stakes, if necessary, to secure the fabric to the ground and cover the fabric with a layer of newspaper or cardboard to prevent weeds from sneaking through.

7. Fill the prepared frame with soil or a potting mix of your choice! Use a rake or the edge of a flat spade to level the surface.

8. Plant! Populate your new raised garden bed!

Planting Your Beds – Tips and Tricks

Building the raised garden beds has finally been done and dusted, and you're now eager to get your hands dirty again — this time, to populate those beds! As with most things in life, there are some techniques, tips, and tricks worth knowing before getting started. Let's dig in!

Intensive Planting

This technique is all about filling up all the gaps so that there is no room for weeds to pop their heads out of! Intensive planting is simply a fancy way of saying you should plant your seedlings closer together. Plants that are happy with intensive planting are the typical greens — mustard greens, lettuces, spinach, and arugula.

Succession Planting

This is a tip for maximizing your yield and increasing the productivity in your garden. Try to plant something every time you dig something up. When you harvest a row of lettuce, plant something in its place; don't leave empty spaces for weeds to crop up and hoard nutrients and moisture. This is a good habit to foster. Before you know it, whenever you dig up a plant, you will automatically be adding compost to the spot and planting the next!

Plant Supports

If you're planting anything that likes to stretch itself over the ground, give it some vertical room to stretch up onto instead. For example, instead of planting cucumber or squash and letting it run around the garden bed in a tangled mess, train it up a lattice or a fence. This makes room for other plants in the garden bed.

Place Beds Away from Trees

After all the hard work you've put into building a raised bed with nutrient-rich soil, the last thing you want is for tree roots to find their way into your garden bed and steal all the goodness from your raised bed residents! Lining the beds with fabric or strong plastic does help to prevent this, but placing your beds as far away from trees as possible in the space you are working with is advisable. Beware of shrubs, too — their roots are just as intrusive as the trees'! As an estimate, plan your raised beds to be positioned a distance of about two or three times the tree or shrub's canopy.

Lining Raised Beds

If you absolutely must place your raised garden bed close to a tree or shrub, the best you can do to prevent their roots from sneaking into the beds is to lay a strong galvanized steel mesh as a lining for the garden beds. At a minimum, opt for plastic or landscaping fabric. Note, laying plastic runs you at higher risk of waterlogging your beds when compared to steel mesh, but if you are careful, plastic or fabric can still be a great alternative.

Best Placement, Sizes, and Layouts

Rules of (green) thumb: the optimal raised bed width is 4 feet (1.2 meters); keep beds short enough that you aren't tempted to hop over them. Eight feet (2.4 meters) is a common length. You generally want to grow beds for flowers or fruits and vegetables in full sun. Also, the most practical layout is a grid formation, giving you easy access to all the beds.

How to Fill Raised Beds

Suppress grass or weed growth by first mowing down if necessary and then laying down a layer of cardboard or newspapers at the very least if you choose not to use landscaping plastic, fabric, or mesh. A standard recipe for garden bed soil is 40:40:20 of topsoil, compost, or well-rotted manure and rough drainage material like bark, vermiculite, perlite, etc.

> **Pro Tip:** If you are constructing a deeper raised bed, consider filling the bottom portion of the bed with old decaying wood, branches, and other compostable biomass plant material. This method is called Hügelkultur and provides your garden with many long-lasting benefits, such as enhancing the soil by adding nutrients and improving its water-holding capacity. The bonus is that you won't need as much soil or compost to fill your raised bed! It's a win-win!

Protecting Plants

The eagerness of the enthusiastic gardener to tuck promising seeds into an early bed can have devastating results. Spring is very much the wolf in sheep's clothing — nothing is as merciless as spring on a gardener's hopefulness. Your tender young greens are likely to face drying winds, chilling frosts, and drowning rains that will tear them down to the earth they sprung from. Certainly, you have no command over the weather, but still, there are steps you can take to protect your precious plants from the fouls of spring. Here we take a look at some measures you can put in place to safeguard your plants from the terrors of the outdoors!

Walls and Fences

The idea of using walls or fencing to protect plants from wind is to decrease the wind speed, not to eliminate it. Bearing this in mind, enclosing your raised beds in slatted fences or fences with open weaves, bamboo fences, wooden picket walls, or fabric walls all allows airflow to your plants while still reducing wind speed in the event of gusts of strong wind. Your barrier should ideally be of a density of 50%.

Living Curtains

If you have a little more room to work with, strategically planted trees and shrubs act as a green physical barrier to strong winds. Tightly grown shrubbery is referred to as "hedgerows," translating in Japanese to mean "living curtains." A living curtain offers the advantages of privacy, snowdrift protection, aesthetic value, and erosion control in addition to the prime value of wind shelter. A belt of up to three rows of trees makes for an adequate windbreaker. You may choose between either evergreens or deciduous trees or a combination of the two. It is recommended that evergreens be planted anywhere from 5 to 15 feet (1.5 to 4.5 meters) apart, while deciduous trees are recommended to be spaced between 5 to 20 feet (1.5 to 6 meters) apart. Shrubs may be planted between trees to fill in the gaps.

Divert Run-Off Water

The amount of run-off water you have in your yard depends on several factors, for example, the amount of non-permeable surfaces in your space. Run-off can wash away your soil and carry nutrients away from your plants. There are several solutions to managing run-off water. One of the simplest is to dig a shallow moat around your raised bed perimeter to retain as much of the soil's nutrients as possible. You can also make a narrow trench to prevent pooling and to direct the excess water off to the side of the raised bed.

Terracing

Terracing is an ancient solution for gardening on a slope. This method involves preparing strips of garden bed horizontally along a slope, lessening erosion and allowing for water absorption. It is important not to leave bare soil with this method, as plant roots help prevent soil from being washed away. Once you harvest, make sure to plant something. Terracing your raised beds allows water to run down the slope and settle in the beds before draining down the slope to the next bed, allowing each bed to be saturated on the embankment.

Garden Mulch

Erosion caused by rain and wind can be greatly reduced with a healthy thick layer of organic matter, either in the form of bark, leaves, straw, wood chips, gravel, or other plant material. Mulch will prevent your soil from being washed away in heavy winds and storms and also protects the surface of the garden bed from pounding raindrops, causing the soil to splatter onto plants, which is unsightly, destructive, and can contribute to the spread of disease. Not only does mulch protect against erosion, but it also acts as insulation, so be careful of how much you use!

Cover Cropping

Cover crops are crops grown for the purpose of covering the soil rather than for harvest or aesthetics. Idle soil, or empty beds, invite trouble into the garden. Cover crops are important for erosion control and protect your soil from nutrient leaching, compaction, and quality deterioration. Cover crops suppress diseases and weed growth, increase water infiltration into the soil, encourage nutrient recycling, fix nitrogen from the air into the soil for the next crop, increase carbon capture, and improve microbial biodiversity. Good cover crops are **grasses** to enhance phosphorus recycling (also great for attracting pollinators), **legumes** for nitrogen-fixing, and hardy, fall-planted species like **winter rye**, **fava beans**, and **hairy vetch** to build soil fertility for the spring.

Garden Bed & Individual Plant Protectors

A gusty wind or a sudden chill runs your plants at risk of damage. Physical protection is available either for the entire garden bed or for individual plants. Cloches are transparent protectors made for individual plants, and they are handy if you only protect selected plants in a bed. However, for complete bed protection, raised bed hoops attach to the walls of your raised bed to create a structure where you can drape any material of your choice over the hoops to keep your plants safe and snug in their beds.

Maintaining Beds

Once you get your garden off ground level and into raised beds, the work's not over! Maintaining your beds is crucial for continued healthy growth and, in the case of a food garden, for a bountiful harvest. Maintenance of raised beds is easier than in-ground gardening.

Watering

Raised beds are great for drainage, but the downside to the fantastic drainage is that they consequently require regular watering. The method of irrigation you select will depend on the orientation of your garden, but usually, drip irrigation works out being the best solution. Overhead watering should generally be avoided wherever possible as this spreads disease.

Mulch

Again, easy drainage means that you want to keep your soil moist for as long as possible. Mulching your raised beds allows the soil to hold moisture for a longer period, so your plants don't get parched. Slow water loss by covering the surface of the raised bed with plant material like wood chips, bark, hulls, grass clippings, straw, or even newspaper or cardboard. Some garden centers sell rubber mulch which does have its pros and cons. The pros are that they last virtually forever, and are low maintenance. The cons are that it is not natural and that they may leech chemicals into the soil. Even store-bought wood mulch may contain chemicals that are undesirable to your soil and plants. If you choose to go with rubber or store-bought mulch, it's advisable to only use them on non-edible plant beds such as flowerbeds or landscape layouts. Stick with natural, organic mulch as listed at the beginning for your fruit and vegetable gardens.

> **Pro Tip:** Laying out landscape fabric on top of your soil before planting is an easy way to control weeds. Just cut slits or holes at the desired spacing — depending on the plant — and sow your seeds or transplants in the openings. You may choose to mulch on top of the fabric, but it is completely optional. This method is gaining popularity in both small and medium-scale farms and gardens.

Weeding

You can mulch your raised bed to the T, and still, there will be the rogue weed or twenty. The thing about weeds is that they are sneaky, and even if you take every measure to prevent them, they do wind up finding a way into your raised beds. However, the good news is that they will be few and far and easily plucked out by hand whenever you have the inclination to do so. Do not allow weeds to grow large and set to seed for obvious reasons! One solution, called occlusion, whereby you spread something over the earth that excludes light and inhibits growth[7]. In this case, we lay the black tarp down over the garden at the end of the gardening season and leave it there until the spring when you're about to sow or plant. Remove the tarp, pull any lingering weeds and sow or plant immediately.

Settling Soil

Regardless of the soil composition that you fill your raised beds with, some settling is certain to occur. As the soil mixture is moistened and the particles fall into place more tightly, some surface soil is lost to tools, wind, and moving plants around. You will have to supplement your garden beds from time to time. Adding a mix of compost and some clean soil will do wonders for your garden bed.

Raised Bed Ideas/Types

Just like there are many materials to choose from to build your raised beds, there are also many types of raised beds to build! Here we explore some popular types of raised bed planters and their benefits.

Built-In

With built-in raised beds, you are building an immovable planter. This is a permanent garden feature and a fixture that can increase the value of your property. Consider building a bench next to your planters for relaxing and sipping on a cup of tea as you watch your plants grow.

Galvanized Sheet Metal Raised Beds

The benefit of sheet metal beds is that the metal acts as an excellent heat transmitter, allowing the sun's warmth to transfer to your plants' roots quicker than other materials — great news for heat-loving plants like lavender and sage. Also, sheet metal is easy to form into various shapes with little effort. Ribbed materials such as culverts are a popular choice. These tend to be thicker and more rigid and can generally be assembled without extra supports.

Square Foot Raised Beds

This is what it sounds like — a grid of square foot sections of growing space (approximately 30 cm squares). The square foot gardening method is appealing to the eye and allows you to grow more variety in the garden as you can have different soils in all the little squares. Simply mark off 12 inches (30 cm) along the top edges of the raised bed walls. Staple or nail string or twine back and forth to the opposite side of the bed and repeat on the perpendicular side of the bed to make a grid over your garden. Now you have individual square partitions ready for planting.

Hoop House Raised Bed

This is like a little greenhouse — a few hoops (or arches) fixed onto your raised bed walls and a protective sheath fixed onto the frame is all you need. This makes for a wonderful all-season garden, enabling you to control even more of your plants' environment!

Also, the critters and creatures won't be able to just nick your veggies anymore! Your plants are completely protected from the harshest weather with this type of raised bed. Shade cloth can also be used over the hoops to protect your sensitive plants from the scorching sun during the hot summer months.

Raised Bed Border

If you're dealing with steep sloping land, raised beds are a simple way to work with what you have to create an illusion of flat land. The layered look is rather attractive and offers plenty of opportunities to play with the texture, color, and framing of the garden.

Trough Gardens

Animal feeding troughs make for great planters — durable, ready-made, large, and movable. Raised bed gardening doesn't get any easier than this. Of course, remember to drill in drainage holes and keep an eye on soil moisture — the troughs can dry out the soil rather fast on hot days!

Raised Bed Arbor

Create a fairytale in your garden with a simple arbor, constructed with trellis or fencing between raised beds. Not only is it beautiful and exciting, but it is so much easier to harvest cucumber, squash, passion fruit, and beans when gravity is on your side! Making use of all that vertical space along the raised beds is a smart way of keeping vining plants off the ground!

Concrete Block Garden

Few building materials are recycled as planters as much as the good old concrete block. They are easy to lug around, easy to stack up, and can even be customized with colorful paintwork. You can come up with some unique bed designs too! A word of caution: concrete blocks do leech lime and consequently raise the pH of the soil over time as decomposition of concrete is usually slow. Seal the blocks with concrete sealant and polymer paint before adding dirt, as this will give you that extra bit of protection and peace of mind.

Tiered Raised Bed

Tiered raised beds typically conjure up images of strawberries tumbling off of the tiers. Tiered beds are attractive and make for great garden features while being functional and practical at the same time. They make use of vertical space, which is always a bonus, and allow for excellent airflow, easy harvesting, and an interesting visual.

Sunken Raised Bed

It sounds like an oxymoron, but actually, this is a clever way to make for a spectacular garden. Instead of raising your garden beds, you could switch things up and dig up the paths. The advantages of a "valley" bed are that they tend to have more accumulated water, are richer in organic matter, and boast more biodiversity. Of course, all this depends on your particular piece of land, your wants and needs, and the soil quality, as mentioned in Chapter 2. If it's doable, the finished look could be worth the immense effort and the masses of soil that will be removed!

Mistakes to Avoid

Gardening is no different from every other venture in life — mistakes can happen. Some raised bed gardening mistakes are pretty difficult or costly to remedy once they have been made, while others may cost you time and patience. Fortunately, we're going to warn you about the biggest mistakes to avoid making so that you don't have to learn about them first-hand!

Beds Are Too Wide

Too wide of a raised bed means you won't be able to comfortably reach the center of the bed. This means you will be stepping into the beds and compacting the soil, defeating some of the purposes of a raised bed garden! Make sure that you can reach every nook and cranny of your garden bed without any ninja skills. Three to four feet (0.9 to 1.2 meters) wide is the sweet spot here.

No Irrigation Plan

This is one of the worst mistakes to make, unless you're keen on winding a hose between your beds and winding it up again — or worse still, walking around to each plant and offering it a drink. No matter what you do to the soil, your plants will be limp and likely perish if you don't give them adequate water. Ensure that beds are near a water source and figure out how you will be watering the beds when you are planning your garden. Bear in mind that in the sweltering summer, you may even have to water twice.

Unsafe Material

Some materials have some ugly chemicals in them. And by ugly, I mean potentially harmful to your health. As mentioned earlier in this chapter, avoid using wood that has been pressure-treated (PT) before 2003. The same goes for using pallets. You'll notice most will have the "HT" (heat treated) stamped somewhere on the pallet[8]. This means it should be free from chemicals, but there may be other identifiers on it. A little research could save you a lot of trouble. Check the safety of any material before you use it in the garden.

Soil Lacks Nutrients

From the experience of many when it comes to dirt, the most successful gardens usually grow from soils that have a healthy dose of organic matter and a bit of your garden soil. Of course, you don't want to use anything that may be contaminated. Potting soil alone will not have enough substance for a raised bed. The benefit of building your soil is that you know what's in it, which means you won't load your tomato and pepper beds with tons of nitrogen, for example. Starting with high-quality soil is important, and maintaining the nutrient load in the soil is an ongoing process. Refer to chapter 2 for an in-depth, step-by-step guide to soil preparation.

Beds Are Too Close Together

How will you keep the grass between your beds short if you can't fit the mower through? Sure, a pair of scissors will fit, but the growing season may be over by the time you're done trimming the grass. Also, wouldn't it be great to push a wheelbarrow between the beds, collect your harvests or throw in weeds and cuttings as you prune? Best of all, wouldn't you like to fit a stool or a comfortable wide crate to sit on as you tend to your little green friends? Yes, the room between your raised beds needs planning! Ideal paths are generally between three to five feet (0.9 to 1.5 meters) wide.

Neglecting to Mulch Raised Beds

Mulch, mulch, mulch. Yes, maybe you're getting bored of hearing it by now but not mulching is an easy mistake to make. The mulch you place in your raised beds acts almost like a cozy blanket for your plants, regulating the temperature of their roots and keeping the moisture from evaporating into the air. Of course, weeds will love the rich soil of your garden beds as much as your plants will, so you have to hinder their growth as much as possible.

An assortment of vegetables in a raised bed garden.

A tiered raised bed on a slope with a hinged "hoop house".

5

VERTICAL GARDENING

A Trendy Alternative

Got the seeds and the soil but short on space? No problem! Of the many gardening methods, there is no doubt that vertical gardening produces the most interesting gardens. It is a method that is plenty of fun and offers tons of room for creativity. The ways you can use vertical space are exciting and unusual. Apart from being so much fun to work in and attractive to look at, the vertical garden offers great rewards in many other ways!

Benefits of Growing Plants Vertically

Vertical gardening offers a multitude of advantages for the gardener of every skill level. Here we explore the many benefits you can reap from a vertical garden.

1. Grow More in Less Space

Helping your plants to reach for the sky encourages healthy growth and more yield in tight spots. You only need enough room for the stem and roots of your plant on the ground, and the rest is taken care of. Lifting plants off the ground opens up more room for other plants to be grown in close proximity.

2. Make Use of Otherwise Unusable Areas

Vertical gardening enables you to grow an assortment of plants in areas and spaces that traditional gardening methods would consider unusable. For example, walls and fences become more than protective barriers — they become potential growing supports!

3. Healthier for Plants

What makes a healthy plant? An extensive root system to soak up water and nutrients, big leaves to grab the sunlight, and strong stems to transport water and nutrients from the roots to the tips of the leaves. The result will be fat and juicy fruits and veggies.

Vertical gardening takes the strain off the plant by supporting it in roomy, airy space, allowing the plant to photosynthesize and fruit in peace!

4. Makes for Simple Harvesting

As if all that isn't enough, harvesting is even simpler when your fruits and veggies are suspended in the air! No more snooping around the ground, peeping under leaves, and watching your step so that you don't squash your plants beneath your shoes. Gravity becomes your friend when you garden vertically.

5. Increased yields

Plants are clever little things. It is almost as though they sense that they have unlimited room and flourish when allowed to extend their vines skyward. The masses of leaves you see above ground are a good indication of the healthy root system the plant has beneath the ground. All that lush foliage and strong stem growth give way to a bountiful harvest!

6. Plants Less Prone to Disease

Lifting your garden off the ground and into the air helps keep plants healthy as they are distanced from the soil, where they would otherwise be prone to disease, rot, and pest infestation. Closer to the ground, leaves smother other leaves and plants, soil splashes onto stems and foliage, pests easily crawl up onto the plants, and there is limited airflow.

7. Increased Exposure of Leaves to Sunlight

With the height of vertical gardening, you can extend the plants onto vertical supports so that the leaves won't overlap. This means that leaves are given more room to soak up the sun and make for a stronger and happier plant. Happier plants equal happier bounty!

Different Ways of Growing Vertically

The gardening terms for the various vertical support structures may appear intimidating to the beginner, but the concepts are simple. Here we dive into the different techniques available to grow vertically, taking your gardening to the next dimension!

Climbing Plants Supports

This is a brief look at some of the many support structures to choose from for your vertical garden! These supports can be handmade from items found around your home or even local yard sales or farmers' markets. Of course, manufactured supports are found at most garden centers or online, too.

Trellis

The traditional technique for vertical gardening — training vining and climbing plants up onto a trellis. Trellises can be any growing support — an obelisk, pergola or an arbor, or anything else. However, when referring to trellising, the reference is usually made to flat structures that are either freestanding or secured to planters, walls, or fences.

Arbors

These are the fairytale structures that transform a regular garden into something magical. Arbors can be arched or squared, have an exquisite entryway feature, or even strategically positioned along a path. Arbors are eye-catching. Some latticework is usually attached to the sides to offer spaces for plants to dig their 'fingers' into as they grip and climb their way to the top.

Teepees

Perhaps the easiest vertical supports to put together. Teepees can be made from many things, even simply a couple twigs off of a tree. Using just wood, metal, or garden stakes, you can make the traditional three-legged teepees as rustic and simple or as intricate and permanent as you like.

Pergolas

Pergolas make for the most incredible seating areas. The lush rooftop of leaves and blooms is quite an exceptional experience, and you can build a pergola to fit your space, no matter how large or small. The canopy of the pergola soaks up the sun while you enjoy the shade beneath. A pergola is a smart way to make your plants work to offer privacy and a shady hideaway in your space.

Arches

Several arches together make up a pergola, but a single arch alone serves as a fabulous architectural feature in the garden. Large or small, arches double your growing space. Growing your cucumbers or squash on an arch frees up the ground beneath it to plant lettuce, arugula, or baby spinach, for example.

Obelisks

Similar to the simple teepee but differing by their four sides, obelisks are vertical structures that are more formal. It is not uncommon to find round-based obelisks as well. These structures are fashioned out of anything from twigs and vines to wood, plastic, and metal.

Cages

Plant cages come in many shapes and sizes — small and short, tall and narrow, wide and short, wide and tall. They are made as simple or as complex as required, from the simple thin cage for supporting a bush tomato plant to the sturdy heavy-duty cages to support vining melons. They may be circular or square, made from leftover materials like fencing and twine, or more intricately fashioned, from wood and wire.

A-frames & lean-tos

These are simple vertical supports made from wooden or metal frames and twine or fencing. Lean-tos and A-frames are very similar, with the latter shaped like the letter "A" and the former simply leaning to one side. A large lean-to frame allows vining plants to amble along with the structure without much training, while there is enough room beneath the frame for a sun-loving mini crop.

Vertical Container Gardening

Planting upwards gives you exponential room to play with; your limit is the length of your plant's green and vining arms. Growing your plants in pots means that their root space is limited, but so long as you feed the soil well and secure good support for the plant to reach up into, you have every chance of success in your favor. Time to take gardening to new heights!

Tower gardens

Tower gardening is a way of using structures like stacked planters or containers, PVC pipes, stacked cinder blocks, stacked tires, or even a long cylinder of wire fencing. The tower is filled with growing medium, and several holes are made along with the tower, from which your plant grows. Popular tower garden plants are strawberries, lettuce, and potatoes. For edible tower gardens, avoid materials such as rubber tires or bare concrete blocks that can leach certain toxins into the soil over time.

Hanging Gardens

You can enjoy vertical gardening without even using up floor space! If you have a sunny wall, take advantage of it by securing hooks and hangers to the wall to hang your planters, from which your plants can tumble out freely in the open air. Hanging pots from hooks attached to the roof of a balcony or deck, or a beam, allows you to grow food out of attractive containers from above. Tomatoes are particularly fond of tumbling from hanging pots!

Living Wall Systems

Living walls are getting plenty of attention these days. They are just what they sound like — walls of lush green foliage and happily flourishing plants. Grown in pockets or on trellises, living walls are excellent air purifiers, offer climate control for buildings, act as noise insulators, promote healthy indoor living and outdoor aesthetic, add fire resistance to your space and increase biodiversity.

Living Art Picture Frames

Indoors, you can grow ferns and low-light loving plants in a shallow planter on the wall, framed elegantly for a classy and stylish vibe. Outdoors, you can play with living frames by placing picture frames filled with plants on your patio table to decorate the space in keeping with the garden theme. Succulents make for interesting and low-maintenance living frames, with minimal watering and soil requirements. You could even place your planters behind an eye-catching frame for an unusual visual!

Freestanding Vertical Gardens

Freestanding gardens are all about no commitments. They are movable, and the plants aren't rooted to the ground. A freestanding system is a vertical garden of planters and pots that you can place anywhere in your space. They are made from shelving, pallets, ladders, wire racks, cleverly fitted gutters to rails, etc. This is an opportunity to get creative with materials and structure!

Best Plants for Vertical Gardening

Finding success with a vertical garden isn't just about the planters and the supports — selecting the correct plants is crucial. No amount of preparation will help if you wind up selecting a plant that simply isn't compatible with vertical gardening — it would be a waste of resources. Imagine picking a bush bean cultivar, for example, and planting it along the perfect lattice, then realizing that the plant simply won't climb! The key is choosing sprawling, vining, and rambling plants — the kind that will take advantage of every support you throw at them! Remember, vertical gardening follows many of the same principles of traditional gardening — your crop-producing plants still need their dose of sunlight!

Popular Vertical Garden Veggies

When it comes to vegetables, a vertical garden lends itself well to indeterminate tomato cultivars, climbing peas, vining cucurbits, rambling melons, pole beans, sweet potatoes, and several varieties of squash. Here is a list of the varieties that are most popular in vertical gardens for each of these veggies:

- ❖ **Cherry Tomato**: Sungold, Gardener's Delight, Black Cherry, Blondkopfchen.
- ❖ **Green Bean**: Meraviglia Venezia, Romano Italian, Gold of Bacau.
- ❖ **Cucumber**: County Fair 83, Saladin, Burpee Hybrid II, Dasher 11.

- ❖ **Melon**: Tigger, Delicious 51, White Wonder, Delicious 51, Yellow Doll, Sleeping Beauty.
- ❖ **Lima Bean**: King of the Garden, Doctor Martin.
- ❖ **Pea**: Garden Sweet, Maestro, Super Sugar Snap, Dual, Sugar Snap.
- ❖ **Squash**: delicata, yellow summer, acorn, zucchini.

Matching Plant Characteristics and Vertical Garden Support Structures

Understanding the characteristics of the plants that you are to grow is essential when selecting the right vertical support structures for them. Trellises are most suitable for lightweight plants with the slimmest fingers — tendrils. Peas and beans wrap onto dainty wires, ropes, or branches tightly as they climb. They don't need deeply anchored supports or sturdy wire or wood — even long branches pushed into the ground by hand would do for these easy-to-care-for plants!

The sturdier the plant, the sturdier the support structure it needs. For example, grapevines are better off with more secure support than you would use for a pole bean or a pea plant. Consider the size and weight of the mature plant when you are planning the vertical support structure so that there aren't any nasty surprises lurking in the future. It's always better to over-prepare and over-plan than to under-prepare or under-plan, especially with vertical structures, which can be a hassle to remove and replace once you have an established and flourishing plant taking over a poorly chosen or designed structure! Plants don't take well to being disturbed!

As practical as they are artistic, espaliered fruit trees are intriguing vertical gardening projects. Espaliered trees are trained on a deeply anchored, solid, and sturdy support against a wall or fence in an assortment of shapes like fans or parallel patterns. Indeed, the harvest is easier, faster, and more plentiful, treatments are applied with speed and ease, and your trees can be fitted into the tightest spaces with this method; however, it is a project best left to the "seasoned" gardener. Espaliering takes skill, patience, and dedication, but it does pay off.

6 Ways to Build a Vertical Garden

If you've decided that you want to dabble in the mechanics of vertical gardening, there are a few approaches to choose from. Whatever approach you take, be sure to choose planters that will accommodate mature plants and to set up a watering system, as containers need frequent watering — more especially with shallow structures mounted on walls or frames. Every space, no matter how small or large, narrow or wide, can benefit from a vertical garden that grabs the eye and rewards in lush foliage.

1. Do-it-Yourself

The only thing standing between your dream garden and the space you have right now is a few power tools and some DIY projects. DIY need not be a project left for those with a tight budget. A successful DIY project instills a sense of pride and can be an enjoyable experience in the garden. Here are some DIY project ideas to get your creative juices flowing:

- Ladder planter - a simple DIY ladder of planters with as many "steps" as you prefer. Looks fabulous casually leaning against a wall!
- Stacked crate design - sun-loving plants flourish in the topmost crates, shielding the shade-loving plants beneath them. Arrange the crates in any design you fancy and color or pattern as desired.

- Hex wire support frame - hanging planters on the hex wire, aka chicken wire, lets you change the arrangement seasonally or as boredom strikes! Plus, plenty of airflow is always a bonus!
- Paint cans & pallets - something as simple as nailing paint cans to pallets makes for a smart-looking and simple DIY project. You can move the arrangement around as you please with ease!
- Tiered baskets - tie together an assortment of baskets with strong polyester rope and hang up on your patio, deck, front porch, or even on a strong tree branch. Makes for an unusual and attractive display of colorful pansies, herbs, and succulents.

2. Prefabricated Trays

Prefabricated trays are popular for vertical gardens primarily because of their sophistication and convenience and the fact that they don't take any floor space whatsoever. Living wall trays are frames equipped with pockets or grids. These trays are installed onto an existing wall and presto — instant vertical garden!

3. Hang-Planters

A few wooden beams secured to a warm southern or western wall make for the perfect set-up for hanging planters. The planters hang attached to the wall in an upright position, offering you a wider selection of plants to grow than compared to tray gardening since you can grow larger plants that prefer more soil than trays allow.

4. Recycled Materials

Tackling vertical gardening projects gives you plenty of reusable and recyclable materials and objects to play with — old pallets, used fences, discarded window frames, empty food tins and bottles, tubs, and sturdy bags, and more. Make sure that if you're hanging material against a wall, you protect the wall from moisture by installing waterproof backing on the frames or vertical structures you repurpose.

5. Wooden Pallets

The gaps between the slats in wooden pallets present the perfect space for filling in some dirt and tucking in pansies, petunias, or herbs. The pallets can be hung on a wall and filled with dirt or hung with planters attached to them. You could also break up the pallet and waterproof or paint the slats to build a customized structure of your own. Food-safe stains and paints are recommended and are usually available at your local hardware store.

6. Existing Nooks and Crannies

A close inspection of your yard will unveil some existing nooks and crannies that lend well to a plant or two. A deep separation in a rock wall holds potential for a flourishing herb. The deep pockets on a palm tree trunk from long-gone leaves are perfect vertical planters for ferns and succulents. Peeping around will uncover some interesting spots for you to get creative with!

7 Steps to Building Your Own Vertical Garden

A striking living wall or tall vegetable support structure is only seven steps away — start building your own today! You may choose to grow in a hydroponic system, in soil, or you may choose to train container plants up a support. Here is an easy seven-step guide through setting up a simple vertical garden piece.

1. Choose a Wall/Plants

The first step is deciding on the finished result and how you imagine it to look. Knowing what you want out of the project is helpful. Is your objective simply to cover up an unsightly wall? Is your aim to grow specific plants and cultivars? Are you choosing a wall for existing plants or plants for an existing wall? If you have a wall to cover up, you have to carefully consider the plants that will thrive in the conditions around that wall; consider the sunlight and the climate and also the wind. If you have existing plants that you want to transplant to train up a wall, choose a sunny wall for fruiting and blooming varieties, and a shady wall for more delicate moisture-loving plants.

2. Choose/Build a Frame

Armed with the knowledge of what you want to plant and where you intend to plant it, you may now begin the actual labor of love — building your vertical support structure! First, choose a material — metal, wood, or plastic. When choosing the material, bear in mind that the structure will likely be moist at all times. Consider the cost of the material, its weight, and its durability. Once you have chosen the material, construct the main frame, but do not attach it to the wall. There are still other elements to be added to the structure before it should be installed on the wall.

3. Attach Backing Layer

The backing layer serves dual functionality in your vertical structure. It acts as a container to form pouches for dirt when opened up. It helps to provide waterproof protection for the wall's surface so that it is not damaged by the constant moisture of the vertical garden. By a small measure, the backing also offers a little insulation, keeping your plants a little cozier in the chill of the night. Be sure to use a tough plastic backing rather than a flimsy kind, as you want the backing to withstand handling, constant moisture, and weathering without tearing.

4. Attach Fabric Layer

The next step is attaching a layer of fabric to the front of the structure. This layer of fabric is what your plants will be tucked into and visible from the front of the structure once it is installed, so choose wisely. While you may use any type of fabric for this layer, it is important for the fabric to have good moisture retention and resilience to not rot with the constant moisture. The most inexpensive materials used for the front layer of vertical gardening structures are felt and canvas. When fixing the fabric to the frame, pull the fabric taut to pull out any creases and screw or staple in place. A staple gun is a handy tool for achieving this quickly and securely.

5. Irrigation and Fertilizer systems

As you will know by now, containers dry out much faster than in-garden beds, which means they require frequent watering. The shallower and the smaller the containers, the more quickly they dry out. Vertical garden structures usually have relatively small pockets, and so they typically require very frequent watering, which can present the gardener with a challenge if pressed for time. Choosing the most labor-efficient and water-efficient method should be a priority. Installing an irrigation system at the top of a vertical garden waters plants from the top down, which essentially means the garden waters itself! If you're hoping there's some way you can make it weed itself, then you're out of luck, unfortunately. Timers come in handy for vertical gardens because the last thing you want is to forget to water your lush vertical garden for a day, only to find it withered and crispy the next (we want crispy fruits and vegetables, not crispy plants!) When setting up an irrigation system, consider setting up a fertilizing system as well, if possible, for the sake of convenience.

6. Attach Frame to Wall

Now that you have constructed the frame, attached the backing and the fabric, and set up the irrigation system, it is finally time to install the structure! The fully assembled structure is easily mounted to the wall but ensure that it is mounted securely. If the structure is a permanent piece, you don't need to fuss over detachable fittings. However, there are advantages to a removable structure, like detaching the structure from the wall to store in a garage, maybe, in the colder months, to protect plants from the bite of winter. Permanent installations will be sturdier in the wind and heavy rains, and if your structure is particularly large, then making it detachable will be impractical.

7. Insert Plants

Now, for the fun part! You may now fill your vertical garden with plants. Create the little pouches for the dirt by making small slits in the outer fabric layer. As soon as you have filled the pouch with dirt and nestled a plant in it, arrange the plant as you like, and then staple the outer fabric of the pouch to the backing to secure the plant to the structure. While it's great if you can staple the fabric as neatly as possible, you don't have to stress over it because your thriving plants' foliage will cover up the fabric front with time anyway. Play with colors and textures of differently sized leaves, and achieve a creative end-product. Putting your heart and soul into the project will pay you off with an attractive feature — a living conversation starter!

A simple vertical garden arrangement.

Vertical Gardening - A Trendy Alternative

An array of flowers growing vertically on vines down an alley.

6

BUILDING YOUR GARDEN IN A SMALL SPACE

Let's Do This!

Look at gardening in a small space as a creative challenge — a fun project to find many ways of growing an assortment of ornamentals and edibles in a limited space. There's an advantage to a clearly defined beginning and endpoint to your outdoor space. You know exactly what you have to work with, not to mention the boundaries that make for an intimate garden. Also, the smaller the space, the more impactful your gardening method and choice of plants need to be. So look out for the bold and the bountiful!

6 Steps for Planning Out and Building a Garden in a Small Space

Understandably, step one is having a vision of the garden you want to create. Your garden has to start on the right foot, and that means you need to know the sort of outdoor space you want to create. Do you want a border? Do you want containers? Do you have walls or fences you want to extend your garden up onto? Is there a specific season you want your garden to be dressed up for, or do you want it to look good year-round? How much time, money, and effort are you willing to spend on the garden? These are all important questions that have to be answered before your journey in building your garden can properly take shape.

1. Choose a Location

Location is key. Location is simply where your garden will be built on your property for optimum functionality. Choosing the location requires some thought and some effort, but it is worth it, as it is a time and money-intensive change to make if you happen to change your mind once you've already built your garden!

2. Where Does the Garden 'Belong'?

If the garden you are building forms part of a larger yard or landscape, you have to choose the right location in the existing space to avoid it looking misplaced. The garden has to "fit in," and the design should flow freely into the space surrounding it. Even the prettiest garden can be an eyesore if placed in a poorly considered location. If your garden doesn't make up part of a larger landscape, you still have to decide which elements of the space will belong to the garden. Are the steps part of the garden? Which walls are part of the garden? Which fences, if any, belong in the garden?

3. Where Will the Garden Be Most Appropriate?

Even if you only have a small space, you need not fill every corner and edge with plants, flowers, and vegetables. You may choose to only garden in half the space you have available, or even less. You need to decide where your garden will make the most sense. Which area will you see the most as you go about your day? Which area will bring you the most joy? If you have a particular spot you tend to sip on a steaming mug of coffee every day, it would make sense for you to build a garden visible from that area or even around it. You may want to garden along a driveway, down a set of steps, on a rooftop, on a porch, or perhaps outside a window for you to view the garden from indoors.

4. Where is the Nearest Water Source?

It's easy to get carried away with spectacular planning and to completely forget about how you intend to water the garden every day. Plants are thirsty creatures, and tottering about with a watering can grow old very quickly. Thus, it is best to either place your garden near a spigot or take the spigot to the garden.

5. What Sort of Background Will the Border Have?

Every breathtaking display has a backdrop, and your garden needs to have one too. A thrilling and vibrant border must have something behind it. Is it a fence? A wall? Is the wall brick or stone? Is the fence wire or picket? Are there tall trees? The backdrop is important to stop your eye from wandering elsewhere and encourage them to focus on the floral display at the border. If there is no background, consider installing one (or growing one — a hedge!) to help your flower border shine!

6. Take Types of Plant You Want to Grow into Consideration

If you already know the plants you wish to grow in your garden, and you are building your garden around them, then you have to consider the specific light requirements of these plants to help plan your garden. You must ensure that the plants that require full sun aren't contending with taller plants, walls, or trees that obstruct their path of sunlight. If you have ferns and shade-loving plants, you have to grow them in areas where they are protected from the harshest rays while still benefiting from bright light throughout the day. Some shade-loving plants are Hostas,

Hellebores, Astilbes, Ferns and Heucheras. Some sun-loving plants are Daylilies, Peonies, Roses, Asters, and Carnations.

Determine Size, Shape, and Layout of the Landscape Border

When building a garden from scratch, you can easily forget that garden borders are an essential feature in the garden's overall look! Here we look at some points to consider when designing a garden border for your space and how to plan it.

Straight vs. Curved Edge

Whether your border takes on a straight or a curved edge will determine how you envision your outdoor space. For a formal garden, your flowers won't be wearing bowties or cocktail dresses, but a straight edge on your borders will deliver all the hard angles that complement formal setups. Formal garden borders are particularly striking when formed into standard geometrical shapes. Curved borders and irregular shapes lend themselves to a casual feel for the kind of garden you want to potter around with a cup of tea. Of course, it isn't a crime to mix and match straight and curved borders — I promise the garden police will be lenient with you! The most important thing is to select the shapes and designs that fit comfortably in your landscape.

Gradual Approach to Building Out/Filling Garden Space

While it is a loose gardening standard that a border's size is in harmony with the size of its surrounding landscape, it can become very overwhelming if you start with more than you can handle. The gradual approach of garden making begins with a small border that is expanded over time. This keeps your gardening experience fun and undemanding, allowing you to deepen your garden borders as time and resources become available. Generally, a four-foot-wide (1.2 m) border is comfortable to start with.

Mark and Measure Garden

It may be very tempting to have an idea of the border you want for the space and to simply grab a shovel and get started, especially if you're excited to get the project started! However, marking out the area you want to dedicate to a flower bed or border and measuring it first is the smart way to go about it. Don't worry, it doesn't require special skills or tools!

Pro Tip: Flip to the *Design Space* at the end of this book to sketch out your garden in a "birds-eye-view" before you break out the shovel. Don't sweat it; the doodles don't have to be perfect. Just having some ideas on paper will really help in the planning stages.

A Few Simple Marking Tools to Help You Visualize the Border

To help you get a real feel for the space, some string and couple stakes, or even a long garden hose, can be useful tools. Simply lay the hose on the ground in the shape you intend your border to be, or use the string and stakes, pushed shallowly into the ground, for straight edges. Once you have adjusted your hose or stakes, step back and take a good look at the "border," walking around the space to get a good look from various vantage points. Adjust the edges as necessary until you're pleased with the look.

Measuring the Space

Once you have marked out the border, use a can of spray paint (white, for easy visibility) to paint a line on the ground to mark out the border. Next, measure the dimensions of the border. When measuring an irregularly shaped border, take multiple measurements by breaking up the border into standard shapes. After collecting your measurements, compare these to the sketch you created in the *Design Space* section at the back of this book. Alternatively, draw your garden and its borders to scale, now that you have physical dimensions. Remember to mark off existing trees, shrubs or plants, and any other objects that may be included in the border, like boulders, fences, walls or statues, etc.

Organize Arrangement/Selection of Plants Based on Garden Design

Once you have put effort into measuring and marking your garden beds and borders, it is only reasonable that you go the whole hog and give the plant selection and arrangement your all, too!

Tall Plants at Back, Low Growers in the Front

Every plant you grow in your border wants to be seen! After all, you wouldn't want your pretty pansies to go through all the trouble of growing those colorful little heads if they're going to be blocked from view by towering dahlias! Make every resident in your garden border feel appreciated and in the spotlight by organizing them in height order. The principle is simple; place the shortest growers in the front, along the edge, and plant in increasing height until you have the tallest plants happily growing at the back.

Color Choice

Countless books have been written on color combinations in gardening, but at the end of the day, the only color combinations that matter are the ones that bring you joy! Your garden border-color palette is a personal choice, and you shouldn't feel pressured by it. Choose what you like and experiment until you find pleasing combinations. Your taste will likely evolve over time, but that's the beauty of perennial borders, anyway!

Pro Tip: As a guide, it's believed that pastel colors (soft shades of **yellow, pink,** or **purple**) are soothing; hot colors (vivid **red, yellow,** and **orange**) are attention-grabbing; and **blue** and **white** shades are neutral colors that don't compete with other shades.

Blooming Sequence

This part will require a little research on your part if you're interested in a garden that is brimming with blossoms throughout the year. Based on the plants you have selected for your growing region or climate zone, you will have to determine the blooming period of each flowering plant you have chosen. Careful consideration can yield you a flowering garden in spring, summer, autumn, and winter. For a budding gardener, managing the blooming sequence of your garden may feel overwhelming, but it sounds harder than it is. Begin by writing down the plants you intend to plant, then the start of their blooming period, followed by the length of their blooming period. Once you have all the information, it's a walk in the park!

P.S. *For your convenience, remember to utilize the blank "Design Space" sheets at the back of this book to help you put your ideas on paper!*

As a guide, here are a few plants for the spring, the long summer and autumn, and the winter. Also included is a shortlist of shade-loving plants that you can grow in the darker corners of your yard to take the most advantage of every little space!

- **Early spring flowering bulbs** – Grape Hyacinth, Crested Iris, Snowflake, Crocus, Winter Aconite, Wood Hyacinth.
- **Long-blooming perennials** – Aster, Yarrow, Bleeding Heart, False Sunflower, Catmint, Daylily, Purple Coneflower, Black-eyed Susan.
- **Winter-flowering plants** – Winter Jasmine, Winter Heath, Christmas Rose, Daphne, Mahonia, Winter Honeysuckle, Pansies.
- **Shade-loving plants** – Lily-of-the-Valley, Primrose, Bleeding Heart, Foamflower, Virginia Bluebells, Hellebore, Lilyturf.

Come Up with a Plan

There's no getting anywhere without a plan. To build the best garden possible in your space, you have to start with the drawing board! Pulling together a vision for the type of garden you want to build in your space begins with some ideas. Even if you already have a picture of what you are looking for from your garden, a little sifting through some more ideas won't hurt! Here's how to develop a gardening plan and how to improve on the plan you have already begun putting together.

1. Find Inspiration

This is where your dream garden begins — inspiration. Find pictures of gardens that inspire you or DIY videos that motivate you. Inspirational garden quotes and images can be clipped, saved, and made as your screensaver on your desktop or mobile device. Find garden projects you are excited about trying or ideas for a private space to enjoy your book outdoors. Whatever your taste, there's inspiration out there, and never before has there been such a wealth of information at every person's fingertip.

2. Look at Ideas from Various Sources

Surf the net, scour *Pinterest* boards, follow gardening legends, and poke your nose around Google's search results. Look at as many sources of gardening information as possible in your spare time.

You aren't looking for your dream garden; you are looking for *inspiration*. Let the fun begin!

3. Collect Items

While the obvious advantage of collecting arbitrary items is that it can save you plenty of money, collecting items for your garden isn't only for penny-pinchers. It is rather enjoyable to find creative uses for everyday objects and breathe life and character into old items on their way to the trash can. It's amazing how practically every object you can get your hands on has the potential to be a container for your plants! A little imagination certainly goes a long way in the garden!

4. Search for Recycled Items to Be Used for Gardening

The most unassuming objects make for charming garden pieces. Scour the antique stores for treasures that can decorate your garden with some vintage character, and *Freecycle*, *Craigslist*, or local thrift shops for some supplies for your small space garden. Garage, yard, or car boot sales can be a gold mine for these items, too. These are all great places to find unique items that will set your garden apart.

5. Household Objects that Can Be Recycled for Container Gardening

Broken crockery, old cans, fish tanks and bowls, bottles and crates, glassware, gutters, laundry baskets, pipes, old baskets, toolboxes, mailboxes, lanterns, jars, damaged watering cans, broken pots — the list goes on infinitely! In fact, the real challenge would be to find a household object that you *can't* use in your garden design!

> **Pro Tip:** Recycling objects isn't as easy as simply selecting your containers and throwing some soil and a plant in them. You should first prepare containers, examine them, and clean out any mildew or rust that may be present. A thorough clean is important to remove potentially dangerous **substances** or debris. Some materials may need a waterproof layer painted on or a latex sealant to protect the container from moisture damage and prolong its lifespan and durability.

Twelve Strategies for Designing a Small Garden

A small space need not be a disadvantage. Don't get caught up with trying to make your small space appear larger; instead, work on maximizing the use of the space to make its unique charm shine. Use your small space for a big and bold display with these twelve simple small-space strategies.

1. Start Small (Pun Intended)

Even in a small space, tackle your garden one space at a time. Give each element the attention and care it deserves until your garden is a thriving mass of blossoms and leaves. Start with the smallest of steps, the least overwhelming, and work your way into your garden projects. One thing at a time! A stunning garden is not the result of a month's work; it is an ongoing and evolving project that you will break down into small tasks.

2. Focus on Using the Garden as a Welcome Space

What better way to be welcomed home than by bright, cheerful flowers, gleefully green leaves, and friendly little shrubs? The space alongside your driveway makes for a wonderful welcoming garden, small enough to be manageable (even for the gardener with the least time on their hands) yet large enough to make an impact. The space along the roadside of your property, or even the area flanking your entryway, all are excellent choices for a small garden.

3. Create a Destination for Eyes and Movement

Even small gardens benefit from gardening principles as applied to large gardens — a focal point, color combinations, and taking advantage of borrowed views and backdrops. Cleverly positioned garden beds with a backdrop of wooded areas can create the illusion of a larger garden. Properly chosen color combinations can draw the eye to spaces you want to make focal points, hold interest, or even make the main attraction. Having a specific garden bed or a nook to catch the eye helps make the garden interesting and engaging. Large richly colored blossoms and unusually colored and textured leaves scream for attention, making for the perfect centerpiece!

4. Incorporate Garden into Overall Structure and Layout of the House

Why not compliment the architecture of your home with a garden? Break away from tradition and merge your garden and your home. There's no need for a large stretch of lawn between the garden and the home. Plant trees, shrubs, and flowering plants around the walls and windows of your home, making it all the easier to enjoy your garden, even indoors, from a comfortable viewpoint! If you aren't big on lawns, you don't need to have one at all! Use your yard for what you will enjoy most.

5. Integrate Modern Conveniences

A barbeque area, patio, or green room can benefit from a small garden border to make the space more enjoyable and pleasing to the eye. An attractive garden bed complements modern outdoor spaces very well. Low-maintenance and slow-growing plants make these gardens even easier to keep. A modern outdoor space can quickly appear cold with all the metal and concrete, so softening the area with a few plants is a clever move.

6. Tie Garden to a Functional Purpose

Plants don't only serve aesthetically. Use them for privacy and even safety. Grow a green privacy screen integrated with a fence to make your yard more secluded as well as natural and less "industrial." Strategically planted thorny shrubs and prickly plants can even act as a security measure around the perimeter of your yard. Planting a green roof or vertical garden across your walls may look pretty but will also certainly reduce your electricity bills by adding insulation. Plants serve many practical purposes!

7. Confine Planting Areas to Perimeter

If your goal is to maximize your lawn space, then a good tip is to keep garden beds to the edges of the house itself and the property's perimeter. Yes, we are talking about the traditional way of gardening, which is the best method if you prioritize your lawn over your garden bed! Many large blossoms can be appreciated from quite a distance, and towering sunflowers will smile at you right from the edges of your property!

8. Keep Things Simple

When you have very little room to work with, sometimes the best way to maximize the wow factor is to keep it simple. This means choosing your favorite plants that will make the most impact and planting fewer plants overall. This avoids the space looking too busy. Use plants to break up the monotony in areas and to introduce some texture in others. Pebbles and gravel of different shapes and sizes can come in handy with this method of gardening.

9. Choose Hardscape Materials Carefully

Limiting your choice of hardscape[9] materials to a single type creates a unified design for a garden that is in harmony despite its limited space. Hardscape materials are the immovable parts of your home's exterior such as stone patios, wooden decks or gravel walkways. The smaller the space, the smaller the plants you should aim to grow, as well, to avoid cluttering the beds and making the area appear unruly or untidy. Limiting the hardscape materials to natural stone and terracotta makes for a nicely unified garden design. Too many different plants and different materials make for a messy finish. Consider the style of home you live in and match the hardscape material that would complement it.

10. Consider the Patio

Gardening on the patio is a wonderful way to join your home to your yard! Every outdoor-loving gardener takes advantage of patio space, if available. Container gardening is the obvious choice, but don't neglect the vertical opportunities to grow beautiful plants! Potted climbers will gladly climb up your patio railing, while current tomato plants will produce heavily in a pot placed in a sunny spot. Hang pots from the ceiling, place a few containers of flowers beneath a table or near the doorway — there's always space for a rooted friend!

11. Grow Vegetables

Vegetable gardening is immensely popular, and for a good reason. Not only do you enjoy flourishing plants and beautiful foliage, but also the visits from sweet little pollinators. Few things feel as good as plucking fresh fruits and vegetables off of your very own hand-reared and home-grown plants! Vegetables are easy to grow and very rewarding, and a vegetable garden is easily grown in any space. Use your fences to train pole beans or cucumbers, and use the bare areas in your flower pots to grow a quick crop of fat radish or frilly lettuce. Don't be afraid to mix ornamental plants with vegetables, either. Break free from the norm and grow your tomatoes next to your roses (actually, the tomato will even protect them from the dreaded "black spot")! Of course, when the bees come buzzing in to taste the flowers, they'll be checking out your delicious veggies blossoms too. It is a win-win!

12. Grow Fruits

If you thought that a small space was a death sentence to your dreams of fruit trees, then think again! Espaliered fruit trees (which I've mentioned before) make for excellent options in tiny gardens. They're easier to harvest and easier to look at, too — absolutely worth the extra effort and skill it requires to grow these trained trees. Fruit trees can be trained along any wall or corner, as long as there is good sunlight to keep the fruits coming! These days, most fruit trees also come in easily obtainable dwarf varieties that you can grow in pots and positions as you please in your garden. Peaches, cherries, apples, pears, plums, so many juicy possibilities!

7

GARDENING UPKEEP & MAINTENANCE

A Little Goes a Long Way

Once your garden is established, and your plants are growing, you can step back and admire all your hard work. However, the work isn't over; in fact, it's far from over. There's still plenty of watering, staking, mulching, fertilizing, pruning, weeding, and cleaning to keep up the beautiful-looking yard! Here you will find all the essential information on maintaining your garden, so it looks its best through every growing season, all year long.

Things to Monitor/Observe as Your Garden Grows

Like us people, gardens age and change over time. Plants grow at various rates, some growing faster than others, some more compactly than others. A newly planted garden bed will require different care than a well-established garden bed. Lawns require reseeding over time, trees and shrubs require pruning or shaping, and the soil needs nutrient replacement. Long-term care is essential for a happy garden. Observe your garden as it ages and perform necessary maintenance to keep it thriving and healthy.

Plants that Need to be Transplanted/ Replaced

The garden bed needs to be reassessed from time to time to check which plants have passed their prime and need to be replaced. Decide which plants have to be groomed a little and which ones simply haven't earned their keep! Overcrowding is never a good look, so thinning out may be necessary as plants grow outwards. Part of checking on the plants is seeing that the beds hold enough interest during every season of the year – you want to have diverse vegetation so that the bed doesn't "nap" all through winter, only to come alive in the spring, for example. If the plants you're replacing are still healthy, consider donating them to a friend or neighbor or perhaps selling them off for some extra pocket money.

Irrigation System Performance

Every plant needs water to grow, and for a breath-taking garden, an irrigation system is a must. Off-the-shelf garden hoses are fine in a pinch, but they may contribute to the spread of bacteria and disease and breakdown over time compared to a properly installed irrigation system. Unfortunately, no water system is fail-proof or fool-proof. This simply means that your irrigation system needs regular inspection and maintenance. Check for leaks, clear any obstructions along the lines, replace worn parts, and adjust fittings where necessary. This is best done once a month.

Soil Health and Compaction

Healthy soil yields healthy plants; there's no way around it. Gardening mistakes like over-fertilizing or improper use of fertilizers, overwatering, excessive use of herbicides and pesticides, and allowing your soil to lay bare or your topsoil to blow off are all contributors to poor soil quality. While halting these practices will preserve the quality of your soil over a greater time, nutrients are naturally depleted from the soil as the plants use them up and as they escape through drainage. Inexpensive soil testing kits are easy to use and help you maintain an excellent growing medium for your garden beds. Avoid soil compaction by growing ground cover crops, mulching, and adding calcium in gradual additions over time. Some types of pruning are thinning, raising (removing lower branches to create headroom), topping (drastic pruning typically done when training trees), and reduction (reducing volume).

Pick the Right Fertilizer

When in doubt, hire the experts. Of course, it's great to add fertilizer know-how to your gardening arsenal, too. Chemical-based fertilizers can easily be improperly applied or used and cause a host of unwanted effects in your garden. Organic fertilizers are usually more forgiving; plus, they'll keep the butterflies and the bees happy, too. Compost teas, well-aged manure, sea kelp, and humates are all excellent choices for a thriving garden.

Pruning for Plant Health vs. Visual Appeal

Pruning is about more than shaping your trees and shrubs. Properly pruned trees open up the canopy to allow better airflow and improved light penetration, benefiting the tree's leaves and any plants growing beneath it. It is important to remove dead, decaying, or diseased growth from trees and shrubs to make room for new healthy growth. Pruning can also deter animal and pest infestation. In fruiting plants, it encourages healthier fruit production. This is a task typically performed on dormant trees, but a little grooming in the summer wouldn't hurt. Keep an eye on pruned trees and keep the soil moist to help the tree recover from the "cut."

How to Save Time on Garden Upkeep

The less time you spend on your knees digging around the dirt (which is very enjoyable in small doses), the more time you can spend sitting back in your green piece of peaceful paradise. Besides, many people are interested in gardening but have very little spare time tending to their garden. Of course, leaving your stemmed friends to their own devices will only leave you an unruly mess to clean up when you do get down to it, so the only way to have a thriving garden with little time to spare is by employing useful tips and tricks in garden maintenance, and that's what this chapter is all about.

Catch Weeds Early in Spring to Avoid Spending Lots of Time Pulling Weeds Later on In Season

Allowing weeds to grow just "until you get the time" to pull them up runs you at risk of letting them go to seed. Once weeds set seed, you are increasing your workload several-fold! Make a habit of pulling them out whenever they catch your eye, and keep a small hand tool within easy reach, so there aren't any excuses to get them right out from the root. Leaving none of your soil bare is a good way to discourage weed growth as well.

The following list includes some of the more natural, organic, non-chemical weed control methods (in no particular order): Landscape fabric, mulching, newspaper or cardboard barriers, tarping, flame weeding, hand-pulling, and organic herbicides.

Vinegar concoctions may work, but they would need to be applied carefully. Some folks have success with it, while others do not. It may depend on the type of weed as well as what stage of growth it's at. Over time, applying too much vinegar may disrupt the soil's ecosystem, thus affecting future plants that you want to grow.

Alternatively, if you are only interested in off-the-shelf weed killers for perennial weeds, a systemic contact weedkiller applied directly to the weed's leaves kills the specific plant down to the root. Residual weed-killers can offer long-lasting weed-growth protection for uncultivated areas. Although these commercially available weed-control methods are effective, they do come with risks. Contact your local garden center for tips on controlling weeds safely and effectively.

Mulch Surfaces to Help with Moisture Retention, Soil Nutrient Levels

A good dose of mulch will do your garden a world of good! A healthy layer of gravel, bark, or organic matter blankets the soil, smothering the growth of unwanted weeds, helping to retain even moisture levels by curbing evaporation, and even improving soil nutrient levels and soil structure.

Watering Crystals and Slices to Help with Watering

Two handy watering tools that you may come to see as a blessing are watering crystals and water slice sponges. The slices are discs of high-saturation sponges that hold large amounts of water within their structure to maintain a moist soil and happy root system in your plants. Some slices can water your pots for up to three weeks long after a single soak! Water crystals are small granules of absorbent material added to potting mix to increase the moisture retention of soil. Increasing your soil's water capacity may not be a good idea for all plants, so it is best to research your plants' needs, as these crystals are not easily removed, as are the slices. Growing your plants in larger pots also means that the pots take longer to dry out and can be watered less frequently. An automatic watering system hooked up to a timer is a gardener's dream, but planting rope in your pots and using the "water wicking" method is an inexpensive way to ensure your plants' soil remains moist. Seep hoses are also handy for even watering that saturates the entire soil.

Opt for Low Maintenance Plants That Don't Require Lots of Pruning and Grow Slowly

This is yet another thing that you may think is obvious, but it is surprising how often this point is overlooked! Fast-growing plants are going to grow unruly quickly and will require frequent trimming and pruning to maintain. Selecting slow-growing varieties may mean a longer wait for the plan to mature, but it also means a lot more time to handle other garden work and tend to other tasks. Choosing plants that suit your climate also reduces maintenance, as you won't be working against Mother Nature herself for the sake of your plants' health! If a plant hates its environment, it will be a mission to make it grow, and that's not the kind of activity you want to be spending so much energy on. Consider drought-resistant, frost-resistant plants, perennials, succulents, and slow-growing shrubs and grasses for a low-maintenance garden. Needy plants and delicate plants are not recommended for a low-maintenance garden.

10 Tips for Keeping Your Garden Healthy

Keeping your garden free of disease can be a challenge. As usual, prevention is better than cure. You can do many things as a gardener to discourage the onset of disease and avoid creating an environment for pathogens to thrive. Diseases occur from three conditions that coincide — a host, a pathogen, and a favorable environment. By eliminating any one of these things, you can keep your plants healthy and strong!

1. Examine Plants Carefully Before Buying

Whenever you purchase a plant, you run the risk of getting a free disease with it. The most practical way of preventing your healthy garden from disease is by making an effort not to introduce disease into your garden beds by mistake. Learning how to tell a healthy plant from a sick one takes a considerable amount of knowledge, but it is worth spending the time and effort to learn. Begin by first learning about your next plant purchase. For example, if you plan to purchase a hydrangea for your garden, scour as many sources as you can for information on what a healthy hydrangea looks like and how to pinpoint possible diseases in these plants. Once you know what to look for, you can carefully inspect plants before you purchase them. For the most part, you will want to avoid buying any specimens that are visibly in poor health, showing signs of wilt, yellowing leaves, rotted stems or leaves, dead spots, or if they are home to insects. While checking the tops of plants is often a good indicator of overall health, it is important to always carefully inspect the root quality of specimens. A less common but incredibly important practice, checking the roots of plants, is about ensuring that they are firm, of even coloring (usually white), well-spaced, and not root-bound. This is done by placing your hand on the soil's surface and holding the plant's stem, then inverting pots to loosen them gently. Ask for assistance from staff at the garden center or the nursery if you are afraid that you may damage the plant or the pot or otherwise make a mess in the store! Don't skip the root check; it is only a matter of time before an unhealthy or ill root system winds up killing a plant or diseasing others!

2. Use Fully Composted Yard Waste

Compost is gold for your dirt. It is a soil amendment that builds your soil structure, helps your soil with water, nutrient and air retention, protects the dirt from drought, helps maintain pH levels, protects from disease, and encourages healthy microbial life. Compost is composed of many types of biodegradable materials, and each of these materials is decomposed biologically at varying rates. Because of this varying rate of decomposition, compost may, at any given time, possess sufficiently degraded material as well as insufficiently degraded material. It is important to note that un-composted material poses a risk of disease to your plants, so using well-aged and completely composted material is vital. This means that you cannot use yard waste as mulch if it has not been properly composted. Also, some materials can degrade the health of your soil if they are applied un-composted (for example, fresh wood bark consumes lots of nitrogen from the soil in order to decompose!).

3. Keep An Eye on Bugs

Not all bugs are bad guys! For instance, ladybugs are more than cute little visitors. They can munch up to 60 aphids[10] a day! Bumblebees, praying mantises, spiders, some beetles, lacewings, and certain wasps are highly beneficial for your garden. Learning to know the good guys from the bad guys helps you create a healthy garden, where good bugs act as natural enemies and assist you in the battle against infestation. Butterflies and bees are among the many pollinators that help your plants reproduce, too. Over 90 plant species relied on for food would be lost without bees[11]! A useful tool for getting a good look at the bugs is a small folding 10-power hand lens.

- *Insect Damage*

The bad bugs do a lot more damage to your plants than what meets the eye. Different insects have different ways of feeding on plants. Damage from insects that have chewing mouthparts is usually visible on the stems and leaves of plants as ragged edges, missing tissue, and holes. Some pests gnaw on the root systems of plants, causing unseen damage to the topmost growth of the plant at first until the plant begins to suffer from the damaged root system, and the visible signs are when it is too late. Damage to roots is commonly caused by cutworm, while common culprits for damage to stems and leaves are caterpillars and grasshoppers.

- *Some Insects Act as Carriers of Viruses*

Damage to roots, leaves, and stems certainly causes stress to the plant, but worse still, insects that cause physical damage to the tissue of your plants leave an opening for bacteria and viruses to infect your plant. Some insects even transport these viruses and carry them from plant to plant! Thrips and aphids are typical virus carriers, as are leafhoppers.

4. Fall Clean-Up

Fall is a time of year when gardeners should be very busy with clean-up. Cleaning up the dead and decaying matter in the yard during fall discourages the spread of disease in the garden. Some diseases tend to overwinter, lying dormant on dead leaves and plant debris in the fall, ready to prey on new growth as it emerges in the warmth of spring. Clearing away dead leaves rids your garden of common diseases, such as "black spot' in Roses, Iris leaf spot, and Daylily leaf streak. You may leave old-growth for visual interest through winter if you are avoiding the garden looking too bare, but be sure to eventually remove old growth to make way for the new in the spring. Keep in mind that little beneficial critters will want to find shelter under those fallen leaves over the winter, which can also provide food for animals and birds when foraging for a meal. A sensible balance may be to do a light raking or mulching around the yard in the fall so that you leave enough shelter for bugs over the winter. In the spring, wait until the ground has fully thawed before commencing yard clean-up to ensure life has been regenerated and off to a good start.

5. Apply the Right Fertilizer

While fertilizers are key for supplying nutrients to all the plants in your garden bed, improper fertilizer application can result in burnt roots or damaged plant tissue. With burnt roots, a plant's ability to absorb water is impaired. Improperly applied fertilizer can do more harm than good, leaving your plants stressed and with reduced ability to fend off disease and the harsh elements of nature. You may think that your plants will use up the nutrients they require from the soil and believe that adding extra won't do any harm, but the fact is that an overabundance of a particular nutrient places stress on plants. The best way to get an accurate reading of your soil nutrient requirements is to perform proper testing. Without testing, you simply rely on guesswork, resulting in unwanted deficiencies and overabundances, even if the fertilizer is applied correctly. Various soil testing kits can be found at most garden centers and other places that sell a good selection of plants.

6. Look for Disease Resistant Plant Varieties

Immune systems are nature's defense force against pathogens. Plants have some form of an immune response, and while their immune systems are not adaptive (like ours), they can still launch self-tolerant responses and establish immune memory. Some plant varieties are specially treated to be able to fight off specific diseases. Looking for disease-resistant types of the plants you intend to grow is a smart gardening tip so that even if your plants get sick, they will know how to fight off the disease without your help. Disease resistance is usually identified by codes on the back of the seed packet. For young plants and seedlings, you may need to ask for help from the gardening staff or fellow gardeners, as disease resistance is not typically displayed on plant tags. A few internet searches or a reference book can help you identify disease-resistant cultivars.

7. Prune Damaged Limbs at the Right Time

The task of pruning is often delayed by gardeners, mainly because it is a very physically demanding activity. Manipulating your plants' growth using selective removal of its limbs is beneficial for healthy growth and to prevent disease. Dying, dead, diseased, or damaged growth needs to be removed immediately, while branches crossing or rubbing against each other and cutting for aesthetics or shape are best done at specific times of the year. If pruning is performed at the wrong time, the plant can be placed under strain or left susceptible to disease. Make a list of the plants that require pruning in your garden and read up on their needs to determine the best time of year to prune them. Below is a helpful calendar for a general timeline for pruning[12].

MONTH	GENERAL PRUNING GUIDELINE
January	- Crapemyrtles - Evergreen shrubs to remove damage - Shade trees - Fruit trees - Grapes
February	- Bush roses - Groundcovers - Evergreens shrubs for re-shaping
March	- Spring flowering shrubs & vines to reshape after blooming - Trees to remove low-hanging, dead, & damaged branches - Overgrown groundcovers
April	- Spring flowering shrubs & vines to reshape after blooming period - Trees to remove lower branches creating extra shade - Fall perennials to encourage branching
May	- Spring flowering shrubs & vines to allow shoots to develop flowers for next year - Shade trees to remove lower branches, creating extra shade - Blackberries by tip pruning canes to encourage branching
June	- Spring flowering perennials to remove spent flowers - Caladiums, coleus, & lamb's ear to remove flower stalks before buds open - Blackberries to remove canes that grow fruit on the ground
July	- Spring perennials to remove dead foliage & spent flowers - Annuals by pinching growing tips from lanky plants - Oaks can now be pruned since Oak Wilt is no longer a threat

August	- Annuals to remove & pinch lanky growth - Perennials to remove spent or dead flower heads - Bush roses to promote new growth and bloom for fall
September	- Perennials to remove dead/dying flower heads
October	- Trees to remove damaged or dead limbs - Shrubs to clean up - Tropical plants need reshaping if moved inside for winter
November	- Trees to remove damaged or dead limbs - Mistletoe can be trimmed from trees - Perennials need to be trimmed to the ground after the first freeze
December	- Trees to remove damaged or dead limbs - Fruit trees to remove vertical shoots - Grapes to encourage twiggy cane growth

As a guideline, warm-weather flowering shrubs and trees are usually best pruned the season before the onset of new growth; plants that flower on the previous season's growth are usually pruned immediately after flowering for best bloom the following season. It is important to use sharp pruning tools and clean the blade with disinfectant to avoid the spread of disease whenever you are pruning. Cut plants back to healthy living tissue and make clean cuts.

8. Choose and Site Plants Properly

Ensure that when you select the plants for your garden and their spots to be planted in, you consider the amount of light the plant will receive versus how much it needs and the soil requirements of the plant compared to those growing around it. It is best to grow plants of similar soil needs together in flower beds so that fertilizing and maintaining pH levels is easier. Make sure that plants that require full sun aren't towered over by other plants, casting a shade over them. Plants grown in conditions other than what they are best grown in are at higher risk of disease and poor growth.

9. Water Properly

Just as your plants love a drink of water, diseases tend to grow just as well with some watering! The many pathogens that threaten your plants that reside in the soil and the air need sufficient moisture to thrive and spread. To avoid creating a moist environment for the spread of disease while still allowing your plants to obtain the moisture that they require, you will have to use watering methods that reduce the chances of water coming into contact with the stems and leaves of the plants. Drip irrigation and soaker hoses are excellent choices for achieving this. To limit foliage exposure to moisture when watering by hand, try to water the ground more than the leaves themselves and water when they have enough time to dry off excess water, like early morning.

10. Don't Crowd Plants

While it can make you very happy to see your plants growing carefree and dense, it leaves a wild and beautiful mess; know that crowded plants are a hotspot for disease. When growth is dense and crowded, the humidity around the plants' leaves increases and creates a breeding ground for pathogens and disease. Powdery mildew, downy mildew, and rust all love this type of environment. Thinning out leafy growth and spacing your plants out well to encourage more airflow is an easy and inexpensive way to avoid the trouble of many diseases. Of course, plants grown too closely together also have to compete for nutrients, water, and light, resulting in poor growth and poor defense against disease. If you feel that the garden bed appears too bare when you supply adequate room for mature plants, then you either have to plant ground-covers, or you have to consider planting young plants closer together and moving them as they grow to maturity. Trimming old-growth and thinning out crowded growth throughout the season ensures the healthiest plants so that everyone in the garden bed is happy!

LEAVE A REVIEW!

If you enjoyed this book, I would be incredibly grateful if you could take a moment to write a brief, honest review. Consider adding a picture or video of your "Design Space" ideas or your real garden with this book to your review!

To leave a review on Amazon, simply click the QR code or link below. OR, search my name or book title by clicking Customer Reviews, then click Write a customer review in Amazon. A review only takes a few minutes and can be as short or long as you like.

https://geni.us/ReviewThisBookOnAmazon

Thank you, and happy gardening!

Jon Marriner

CONCLUSION

Gardening is an exciting, rewarding, and therapeutic experience that can be enjoyed in any space. This book will have proven that to you! There's no better way to spend spare time than by soaking up some sun as you stroll through your little piece of nature or getting down on your knees and playing with the dirt. Approach your gardening from a place of love and joy, and your plants will return the favor!

If you're a beginner gardener, I trust that this book will have motivated you to build a garden in your space (no matter how challenging it may have seemed at first!) and that you have sufficient guidelines to make the journey successful and enjoyable. This book will have steered you in the right direction by helping you make important decisions for the planning phase, then supplying you with the information you need on how to carry out your big ideas in a small space! For the seasoned gardeners, I trust that you have learned valuable tips and tricks on plant care to add to your gardening repertoire and get more out of your gardening experience, with less disease, weeds, and waste! The maintenance advice tucked in the pages is a time and effort saver for any gardener and will ensure that your plants are well looked after for a beautiful-looking garden.

You are now armed with all the best information to grow a thriving garden, brimming with the happiest and healthiest plants — time to get down and dirty! Be sure to *leave a review on Amazon* if you found this book a helpful, informative, and an enjoyable read — everything I intended it to be!

> Let's stay connected!
> You can always find me at our exciting, growing Facebook community and home page!
> www.facebook.com/groups/homesteadoffgridworld

GARDENER'S TERMINOLOGY

This comprehensive terminology reference guide will help you better understand the terms used by gardeners, permaculturists, and horticulturalists alike. Keep it handy!

Acidic: A soil, compost, or liquid with a pH between 0 and 7.0 (on a scale of 0.0-14.0). Often referred to as "sour" soil by gardeners.

Aeration: Any method of loosening soil or compost to allow air to circulate.

Aerobic: Describes organisms living or occurring only when oxygen is present.

Alkaline: A soil with a pH between 7.0 and 14 (on a scale of 0.0-14.0). Often referred to as "sweet" soil by gardeners.

Anaerobic: Describes organisms living or occurring where there is no oxygen.

Annual: A plant that blooms, produces seed, and dies in one year.

Beneficial Insect: An insect that benefits your garden by eating or laying its eggs in other insects, thereby controlling its population.

Biennial: A plant that completes its full life-cycle in two growing seasons. It produces leaves in the first and flowers in the second.

Biochar: A valuable soil amendment dating back at least 2500 years. It is black carbon charcoal produced from biomass sources (i.e., wood chips, plant residues, manure or other agricultural waste products). The carbon material can be mixed in with your soil/compost to charge it with nutrients and inoculate it with microbes. This makes for an excellent soil enhancer.

Biodegradable: Able to decompose or break down through natural bacterial or fungal action. Substances made of organic matter are biodegradable.

Biodiversity: Is the different kinds of life found on earth. It includes all living things, not just the plants and animals that are common or easily seen. It encompasses life at all its levels.

Biological Pest Control: Using living organisms such as beneficial insects or parasites to destroy garden pests.

Black Spot: A fungus that primarily affects roses but can also be found on other ornamental and garden plants.

Bolt: A term used to describe a plant that has gone to seed prematurely.

Bone Meal: Finely ground fertilizer composed of white or light gray bone that adds phosphorus to the soil.

Calcitic Limestone: A common material used for "liming" soil with an acid level that is too high. This type is most commonly used and contains calcium carbonate.

Chelation: The bonds between organic compounds and metals, some of which are insoluble, as in humus. Soluble chelates are used in fertilizers to help keep nutrient metals, such as iron, mobile in the soil and thus available to plants rather than locked up in insoluble mineral salts.

Chlorosis: A yellowing or blanching of the leaves due to lack of chlorophyll, nutrient deficiencies, or disease.

Cloches: Transparent protectors or domes to protect individual plants from cold temperatures.

Coconut Coir: Also known as coir-peat, coco-peat, coir fiber pith or coir dust is fibrous husks of the inner shell of the coconut. Used for lining hanging baskets and mixed in with potting soil to improve air porosity, even when wet, and aids in moisture retention.

Cold Frame: An unheated structure usually made of wood and covered with glass or plastic. Cold frames are used to protect plants from frost and are helpful season extenders.

Companion Planting: The sowing of seeds in the garden so that plants help each other grow instead of competing against each other.

Compost: Completely decayed organic matter used for conditioning soil. It is dark, odorless, and rich in nutrients.

Compost Tea: A liquid fertilizer made by soaking compost in water to extract the nutrients.

Cover Crop: Vegetation grown to protect and build the soil during an interval when the area would otherwise lie fallow.

Crop Rotation: The planting of a specific crop in a site different from the previous year.

Cross-Pollination: When two or more plants of the same species pollinate each other's flowers; for many fruit trees, cross-pollination is necessary to produce a crop.

Cultivar: Are plants you buy that often have been propagated not from the seed but rather stem cuttings, grafting, or tissue cultures to ensure it retains the characteristics of the plant parent.

Cutting: A vegetative method of plant propagation whereby a piece of a plant leaf, stem, root, or bud is cut from a parent plant. It is then inserted into a growing medium to form roots, thus developing a new plant.

Damping Off: Decay of young seedlings at ground level following a fungal attack. Often the result of soil-borne diseases and overwatering.

Dead Heading: The act of removing spent flowers or flowerheads for aesthetics, prolonging bloom for up to several weeks or promoting re-bloom, or preventing seeding.

Deciduous: Plants that lose their foliage during the winter months.

Deep Shade: A plant requiring less than 2 hours of dappled sun a day.

Desiccate: Cause to dry up. Insecticidal soap desiccates its victims.

Determinate Tomatoes: These varieties grow to a fixed size and ripen all their fruits in about two weeks. Once this first set of fruit has ripened, the plant's growth will begin to slow down and will set little to no new fruit.

Direct Seed: To seed directly into the soil instead of starting your seeds indoors.

Double Digging: A method of preparing the soil by digging a trench then putting the soil from one row into the next row.

Drip irrigation: Any type of irrigation in which the water drips out slowly at the base of individual plants; this approach uses far less water than sprinklers.

Dwarf: Plant bred to be smaller than what is typical for the species; fruit trees are often classified according to their degree of dwarfness.

Espalier: The art, or process, of controlling plant growth on a flat surface, usually against a wall or fence or along a trellis.

Evergreen: Plants that retain their foliage throughout the year.

Fertilizer: An organic or synthetic material added to the soil or the plant that is important for its nutrient value.

Foliar Fertilizing: A technique of feeding plants by applying liquid fertilizer directly to plant leaves.

Frost Date: This is the average expected last frost date for your area. Frost dates are important to know for your gardening zone or planting area.

Fungicides: Compounds used to prevent the spread of fungi in gardens and crops, which can cause serious damage to plants.

Furrow: A small trench made in the soil for planting seeds; may also refer to the depression between raised planting beds.

Germinate: The beginning of growth in seeds, the action of sprouting, budding, or shooting, above the soil. This occurs whenever a plant or seed begins to vegetate into leafy young plants. The breaking of dormancy in seeds or the sprouting of pollen grains deposited on a stigma.

Graft: To splice two portions of a plant together to fuse into a solid piece; grafting is used to attach scion (a piece of wood with preferable fruiting or flowering traits) to a rootstock (separate but closely related genetic material selected for desirable root characteristics).

Green Manure: A crop that is grown and then incorporated into the soil to increase soil fertility or organic matter content. Usually turned over into the soil a few weeks before new planting begins.

Hardening Off: The process of acclimatizing plants grown under protection, in the greenhouse, for example, to cooler conditions outdoors.

Hardiness Zones: A system of classifying plants according to the minimum winter temperature they can tolerate; the USDA has developed a map of 26 hardiness zones, defined by 5-degree temperature increments.

Hardscape Material: Refers to the immovable parts of your home's exterior, such as stone patios, wooden decks, or gravel walkways, as opposed to trees, bushes, and the like, which are semi-moveable (since they can be dug up and replanted).

Heavy Soil: A soil that contains a high proportion of clay and is poorly drained.

Herbaceous: Plants that do not have woody stems, only soft green stalks and leaves.

Humus: A fairly stable, complex group of nutrient-storing molecules created by microbes and other forces of decomposition by the conversion of organic matter. Typically, it's dark loamy earth.

Indeterminate Tomatoes: Are traditional tomato plants that never stop growing until disease or weather halts growth. Often called "vining" tomatoes.

Inoculant: A substance containing beneficial soil microbes, commercial inoculants are used for various purposes, from hastening decomposition rate in a compost pile to improving soil fertility.

Integrated Pest Management (IPM): A pest control strategy that uses an array of complementary methods: natural predators and parasites, pest-resistant varieties, cultural practices, biological controls, various physical techniques, and pesticides as a last resort. It is an ecological approach that can significantly reduce or eliminate the use of pesticides.

Iron Chelate: is a soil amendment that corrects chlorosis, a condition characterized by yellow leaves with green veins; iron chelate is available in organic and synthetic forms.

Gardener's Terminology

Loam: Fertile, well-drained soil; loams have an ideal balance of sand, silt, and clay particles, along with abundant organic matter and humus content.

Light Feeder: Crops that can produce good yields on marginally fertile soil; includes most herbs, greens, and root crops.

Micro-Nutrients: Some mineral elements are needed by plants in very small quantities. If the plants you are growing require specific "trace elements," and they are not getting them through the soil, they must be added.

Monoecious: Term for species in which male and female flowers are produced on the same plants, such as squash, cucumbers, and most fruit trees; with monoecious plants, only a single specimen is needed for pollination (and thus fruit production) to occur.

Mulch: Any organic material, such as wood chips, grass clippings, compost, straw, or leaves spread over the soil surface (around plants) to hold in moisture and help control weeds.

Naturalized: Plants that have spread over a large area over time, whether by self-seeding or creeping rhizomes; this is the goal of native plant restoration.

Nightshade: Plants in the Solanaceae family, which include many common vegetables, such as tomatoes, potatoes, peppers, and eggplant.

Nitrogen-Fixing: Plants that form a symbiotic relationship with soil microbes that chemically convert atmospheric nitrogen to a soluble form of nitrogen, the nutrient responsible for the rapid green growth.

No-Till-Gardening: This type of gardening calls for no soil cultivation (or tilling) after the initial tilling. In its place, regular mulches are added, and plants are planted through the mulch.

This saves on labor and eliminates weeds, which might germinate as a result of tilling.

N-P-K: An abbreviation for the three main nutrients that have been identified as absolutely necessary for plants are nitrogen (N), phosphorus (P), and potassium (K). These three are also known as "macronutrients" and are the source of the three numbers commonly found on fertilizer labels.

Occlusion: Using opaque material such as tarp or cardboard to cover the ground will still allow weeds to germinate but eventually die without light.

Open-Pollinated: Crop varieties that, unlike hybrids, produce seed that is identical to the parent plant; heirloom vegetables are typically open-pollinated, which makes it easier to save and replant their seed.

Organic: Refers to something derived from living organisms and is made up of carbon-based compounds. It is also a general term used for gardening using no chemical or synthetic fertilizers or pesticides.

Organic Gardening: This gardening method is based on building healthy, living soil through composting and using supplemental nutrients from naturally occurring deposits. The basic principle is to feed the soil so the soil will feed the plants. Healthy plants are better able to resist pests and disease, thus reducing the need for control. If control is needed, cultural and mechanical methods are used first. Naturally derived pesticides are used only as a last resort.

Perennial: A plant that grows and flowers for more than years. They are either evergreens or plants that may die back to the ground but will grow again the following season.

Perlite: Also known as "volcanic popcorn" is a common ingredient in potting soil. A volcanic mineral that has been heated, causing it to puff up. Perlite has exceptional water and air holding capacity, which helps prevent soil from becoming compacted or drying out.

Permaculture: "The conscious design and maintenance of agriculturally productive ecosystems which have the diversity, stability, and resilience of natural ecosystems. It is the harmonious integration of landscape and people providing their food, energy, shelter, and other material and non-material needs in a sustainable way." - Geoff Lawton

pH: A scale from 0-14 that explains the degree of acidity or alkalinity of the water or soil. Soil pH is very important because it affects the availability of nutrients to plants and the activity of microorganisms in the soil.

Phosphorus: Essential nutrient involved in photosynthesis and various metabolic functions (abbreviated P on fertilizer products); bone meal and rock dust are the primary sources of organic phosphorus.

Pinch Back: To remove the tip of a growing stem, whether with the fingers or hand pruners; this stimulates branching lower down on the plant, encouraging a shorter, bushier growth habit.

Potassium: Essential nutrient involved in various metabolic functions in plants (abbreviated K on fertilizer products); greensand, kelp meal, and wood ashes are the primary sources of organic potassium.

Rhizome: A fleshy underground stem or runner. Creeping grasses are spread by rhizomes.

Root-bound: A plant whose roots have grown into a tight mass inside a pot; plants are healthier and more vigorous when transplanted before they become root-bound.

Scarification: Penetrating the outer layer of seeds to encourage germination; depending on the species in question, sandpaper, files, or other tools may be used to open the hard outer coat of seed so that water may enter.

Season Extender: Any technique or piece of equipment used to extend the growing season in both spring and fall. Examples include; row covers, greenhouses, hotbeds, cold frames, and products such as Wall O' Waters.

Shou Sugi Ban: (Translation: charred cedar board). An ancient Japanese architectural technique that was used to preserve many wood types by charring the surface with a hot flame. Evidence shows this is an excellent chemical-free method that can deter bugs and resist the elements.

Side Dress: Applying a strip of fertilizer along the side of a bed of established plants to maintain adequate nutrient levels through the end of the growing season.

Soil Amendment: Material added to the soil to improve its properties. This may include water retention, permeability, water infiltration, drainage, aeration, and structure. Soil amendments are mostly an organic matter or very slow-release minerals and are typically worked into the topsoil.

Soil Test: A measurement of the soil's major nutrients (nitrogen, phosphorous, and potassium) and pH levels.

Solarization: The process of heating the soil underneath to kill weeds or grass by covering the desired area with a clear plastic tarp.

Stratification: Subjecting seeds to the conditions required to break their dormancy (mimicking the natural processes that they've evolved with) so that germination may occur; the most common form is cold stratification, which involves storing the seeds in a refrigerator or freezer for weeks or months to mimic the winter season.

Subsoil: The infertile layer of soil beneath topsoil that contains minerals but little to no biological activity or organic matter; also called mineral soil.

Tendril: Slender whiplike or threadlike strands of a climbing plant, often growing in a spiral form, stretching out and twining around any suitable support.

Terra Preta: The technique of using charcoal to improve the fertility of soils. Originated in the Amazon basin at least 2500 years ago

Tilth: Describes the general health of the soil, including a balance of nutrients, water, and air. Soil that is healthy and has good physical qualities is in good tilth.

Topdressing: Applying fertilizers or some kind of soil amendment after seeding, transplanting, or once the crop has been established.

Topsoil: The fertile, biologically active layer of soil closest to the surface; topsoil includes organic matter, humus, and a plethora of microbes, earthworms, and insects.

Transplanting: The moving of a plant from one growth medium to another.

Variegated: Plants with multi-colored foliage.

Vermicomposting: The use of red worms to convert food scraps or other organic materials into worm castings.

Vermiculite: A common ingredient in potting soil. Vermiculite is a mica-like mineral that has been heated, causing it to expand into a spongy material with exceptional water and air holding capacity; it has similar properties as perlite.

Wet Feet: The condition of having waterlogged soil around the roots of a plant; contributes to fungal disease in most crops and can kill plants outright.

Worm Casting: The digested organic waste of red worms. Gardeners consider them the most nutrient-dense organic compost available.

Xeriscaping: To create a low-maintenance landscape with native plants and small or non-existent areas of turfgrass. One of the primary goals of xeriscaping is to reduce landscape water use.

GLOBAL HARDINESS ZONES

CANADA & USA

These hardiness zone maps are a general guide only. Please check your local area for your exact, up-to-date zone.

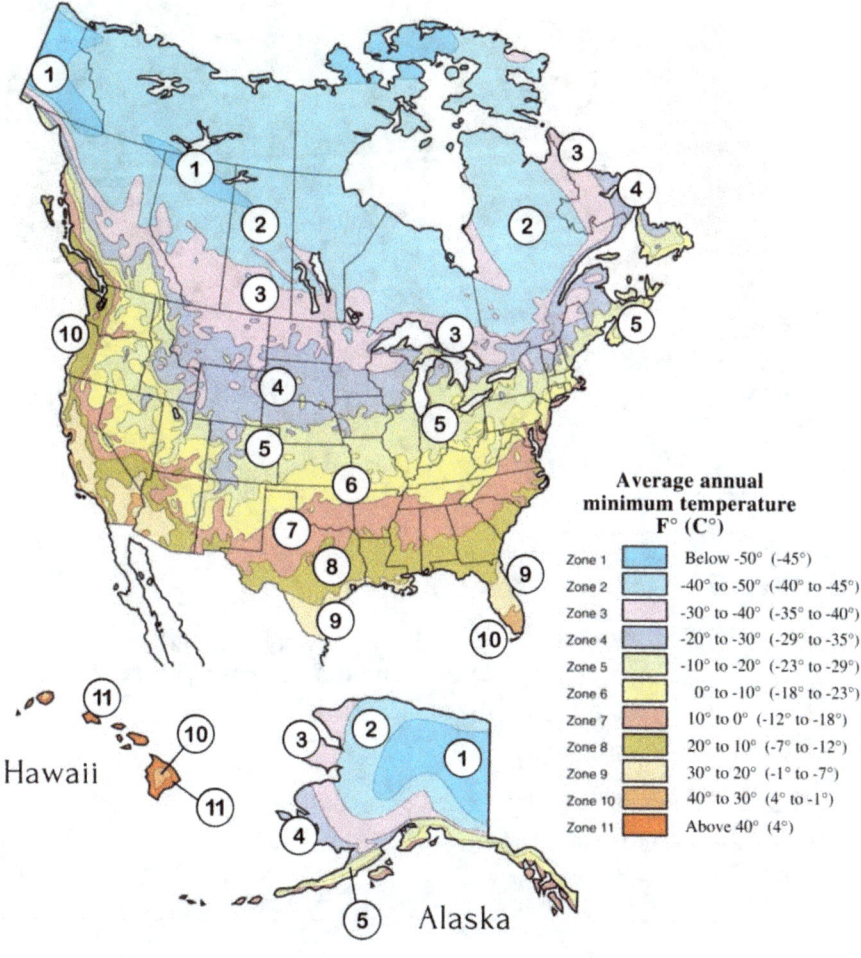

EUROPE

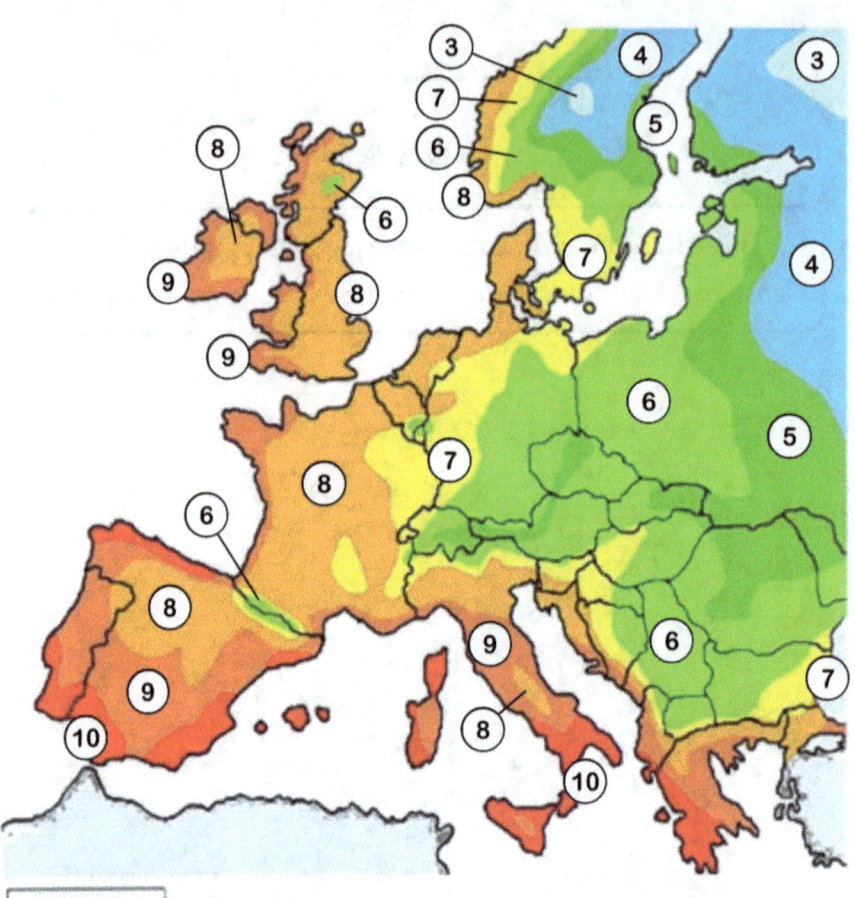

AUSTRALIA

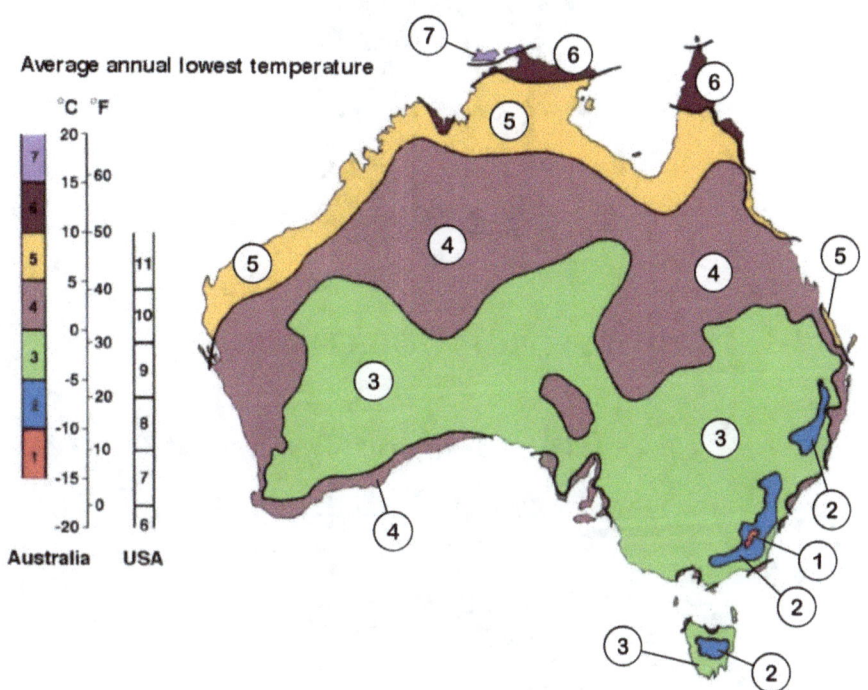

Zones are not the same as the USDA plant hardiness zones.
The "USA" scale shows the USDA equivalents.

DON'T FORGET YOUR FREE GIFT!

Click the QR code or visit my website at:

www.HomesteadOffgridWorld.com

Be sure to join our members-only Facebook community to interact with beginner and experienced gardeners from around the world!

www.facebook.com/groups/homesteadoffgridworld

REFERENCES

CH.1
1. Grant, B. W. (2009). *How strong is the evidence that solar ultraviolet B and vitamin D reduce the risk of cancer?* Dermato Endocrinology.
2. Chang. L. (2004). *Vitamin D: Vital Role in Your Health.* WebMD. https://www.webmd.com/food-recipes/features/vitamin-d-vital-role-in-your-health

CH.2
3. Gardener's. (2021, Jan 17). Sand? Clay? Loam? What Type of Soil Do You Have? Gardener's Supply. https://www.gardeners.com/how-to/what-type-of-soil-do-you-have/9120.html

CH.3
4. Fluegel, J., & Fluegel, S. (n.d.). Find Out the Size Pot You Need for Container Gardening. Grey Duck Garlic. Retrieved October 11, 2021, from http://greyduckgarlic.com/container-gardens.html
5. Sellmer, J., PhD, & Kelley, K., PhD. (2021, October 3). Homemade Potting Media. Penn State Extension. https://extension.psu.edu/homemade-potting-media

CH.4
6. Overview of Wood Preservative Chemicals. (2021, March 5). US EPA. https://www.epa.gov/ingredients-used-pesticide-products/overview-wood-preservative-chemicals
7. Seal, J. (2020, November 17). Can You Lay Black Plastic Directly Over Current Weeds to Kill Them? Home Guides | SF Gate. https://homeguides.sfgate.com/can-lay-black-plastic-directly-over-current-weeds-kill-them-86067.html
8. https://www.1001pallets.com/heat-treated-pallets-want/

CH.6

9. Cooper, K. (n.d.). Types of Hardscape Materials. Hunker. https://www.hunker.com/13580785/types-of-hardscape-materials

CH.7

10. Where Did All These Ladybugs Come From?! (n.d.). Urban Tree Service. Retrieved October 11, 2021, from https://urbantreeservice.com/general/where-did-all-these-ladybugs-come-from/
11. Benjamin, A. (n.d.). Why bees are the most invaluable species. The Guardian. Retrieved October 11, 2021, from https://www.theguardian.com/environment/blog/2008/nov/21/wildlife-endangeredspecies
12. Calloway's Nursery. *Pruning Calendar*. (n.d.). https://www.calloways.com/wp-content/uploads/pruning-calendar-hou.pdf

Gardener's Terminology

Barth, B. (2018, July 27). 100+ Gardening Vocabulary Terms You Need to Know in 2018. Modern Farmer. https://modernfarmer.com/2018/07/100-gardening-vocabulary-terms-you-need-to-know-in-2018/

Planet Natural. (2018, May 4). Gardening Terms (Glossary). https://www.planetnatural.com/vegetable-gardening-guru/garden-terms/

Global Hardiness Zones

Folds, E. (2021, April 7). Get Your Victory Garden Growing With This Planner. Garden Culture Magazine. https://gardenculturemagazine.com/get-your-victory-garden-growing-with-this-planner/

Dawson, I. (2021, January 22). Plant Hardiness Zones for Australia. Australian National Botanic Gardens. https://www.anbg.gov.au/gardens/research/hort.research/zones.html

DESIGN SPACE

DESIGN SPACE

DESIGN SPACE

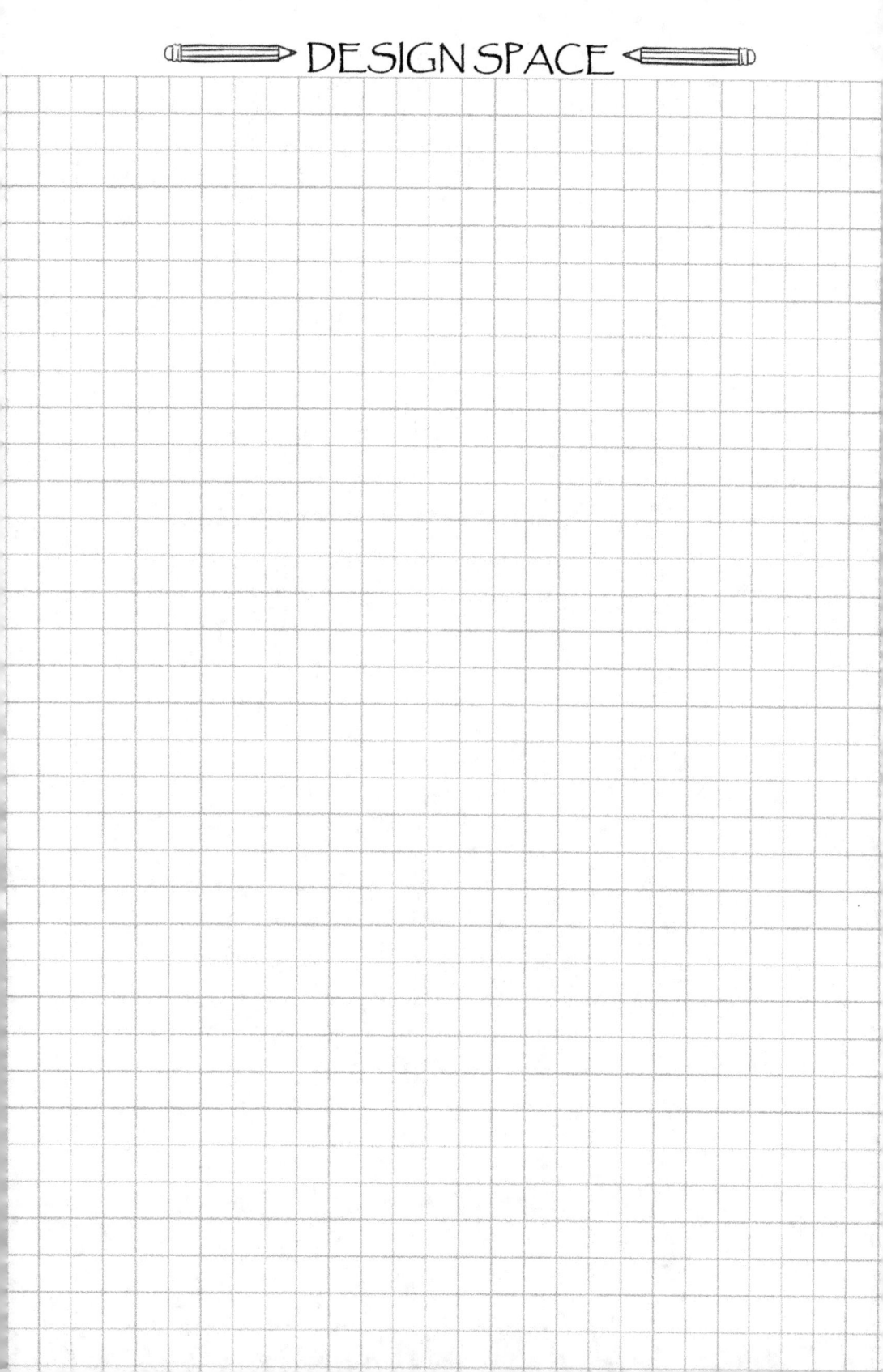

DESIGN SPACE

DESIGN SPACE

DESIGN SPACE

Scan the QR code below for additional Design Space sheets to print out.

www.ingramcontent.com/pod-product-compliance
Lightning Source LLC
Chambersburg PA
CBHW072154100526
44589CB00015B/2230